LEADERSHIP
DIALOGUES

LEADERSHIP
DIALOGUES

CONVERSATIONS AND ACTIVITIES FOR LEADERSHIP TEAMS

JOHN WEST-BURNHAM
AND DAVE HARRIS

Crown House Publishing

www.crownhouse.co.uk
www.crownhousepublishing.com

First published by
Crown House Publishing
Crown Buildings, Bancyfelin, Carmarthen, Wales, SA33 5ND, UK
www.crownhouse.co.uk
and
Crown House Publishing Company LLC
PO Box 2223, Williston, VT 05495, USA
www.crownhousepublishing.com

Pages 82–83: Extract from Sutton Trust-Education Endowment Foundation Toolkit has been reproduced with permission.

Resource A3(iv): Extract from 'A Bravery Pledge' © Lynn C. Johnston has been reproduced with kind permission.

Resource A6(ii) extract from *The Teachers' Standards* under Open Government Licence. Please visit www.nationalarchives.gov.uk/doc/open-government-licence/version2

British Library of Cataloguing-in-Publication Data
A catalogue entry for this book is available from the British Library.

Print ISBN 978-1-84590-906-2
Mobi ISBN 978-1-84590-922-2
ePub ISBN 978-1-84590-923-9
ePDF ISBN 978-1-84590-924-6

LCCN 2014958604

Printed and bound in the UK by
Bell & Bain Ltd, Thornliebank, Glasgow

Contents

Introduction

The purpose of this book is to provide a range of materials and resources to stimulate and support dialogue and conversations between leaders. Leadership work in schools is made up of countless conversations – some brief and fleeting, others far more significant. While we value these conversations as a significant element in the development of all staff, we argue that there is a need for a more structured approach that involves seeing dialogue as a crucial resource in leadership development and learning. In particular, we would stress the importance of leadership teams moving their meetings from the operational to the developmental.

Meetings in school can become focused on the urgent and important. This is perfectly proper and understandable. The danger is that the operational drives out the strategic and, in particular, the team fails to develop as a team through shared learning and professional dialogue. One of the defining characteristics of highly effective teams is that they have a common language based on a shared vocabulary, agreed definitions and mutual understanding. The best way to achieve this is through regular, structured dialogue.

Too often, leaders are side-tracked by the urgent yet mundane. Hours of invaluable leadership team time is taken up with conversations about practicalities and systems, rather than issues that have the potential to make long term differences to the pupils and their communities. This book provides leaders with questions, research, ideas and printable resources around which to base the work of their team. Each resource can be used as it is or adapted to your own personal circumstances. There is no perfect answer, just the right one for you and your context.

This is not a typical book. We don't expect you to start at page 1 and read it in numerical order. This book contains over 40 questions, grouped into eight themes (A–H), that are important to school leaders. Turn to a theme that is relevant to you, identify one of the questions as your focus and you will find that this, in turn, has six elements:

Question

Focus on the full wording of this question.

Why is this important?

Here we include reasons why this is a question you should answer.

Key quotes for the section

Sometimes a few thoughts from another point of view will help you.

Section discussion (CD-ROM)

Our thinking on the topic (available in printable format on the CD-ROM), provoking you to decide what you and your team think on the topic.

Key questions

Some questions for you to answer as a leadership team.

Resources (CD-ROM)

A list of the materials available on the CD-ROM (these are linked to the discussion and will support your thinking on the topic).

Possible ways to use the book

→ Put aside half of every meeting to cover a topic from the book.

→ Dedicate one meeting each month to a theme of key importance.

→ Use the contents as a voting form for the team to make decisions.

→ Choose a topic at random for the team to work on (dart not included).

→ Focus on a combination of themes to fit your situation, which you will need to prioritise – for example:

  → A new leader: F, A, D.

  → Wanting to improve Ofsted grade: D, B, E.

  → Wanting to maintain high grade: B, C, G.

  → Needing to regenerate community: H, G, E.

  → Helping the staff improve: F, D, A.

Instructions for use

To get the maximum benefit from this book, choose a topic from the contents list and print out the dialogue (there is a printable version on the CD-ROM), asking the whole team to read this in advance of your meeting (none will take more than five minutes). Print out the associated resources beforehand and, where indicated, distribute particular ones in advance. This will ensure that your meeting time is used purely for discussion. Prioritise this time. Dialogue is not the icing on the cake – it is the very material from which an effective school is made.

Some thoughts on dialogue

Preskill and colleagues (2000: 88) identify a range of qualities or dispositions that are necessary for effective dialogue and therefore model the essential attributes of shared leadership learning:

→ *Hospitality:* Inviting, engaging and welcoming.

→ *Participation:* The expectation that all will contribute and become involved.

→ *Mindfulness:* Sensitivity and awareness.

→ *Humility:* The recognition that no one individual can have a monopoly on truth or insight.

→ *Mutuality:* Recognition and respect for others.

→ *Deliberation:* Careful and deliberate thinking based on evidence.

→ *Appreciation:* Recognition, acknowledgement and celebration.

→ *Hope:* An optimistic and positive outlook.

→ *Autonomy:* Balancing the needs for individuals to retain their personal integrity while working interdependently.

These qualities and dispositions seem fundamental to any effective relationship, but they are particularly significant in the context of the social relationships that need to exist in order to nurture successful leadership. Although it would be naive to pretend that leadership teams are not highly complex social entities with competing priorities, multiple perceptions and the potential for micro-politics as robust as any Renaissance court, the performance of the team is directly correlated with the quality of its relationships.

It is very difficult to contemplate any team development strategy that does not involve sophisticated levels of dialogue as a key leadership strategy and essential behaviour. Dialogue is more than effective communication; it is about developing significant relationships and enabling effective learning:

> Dialogue ... is an art and a discipline that deepens and grows more meaningful the more we engage in it. Dialogue also gets better the more we try out different moves and experiment with a variety of ways to listen more fully, speak more fluently from the heart, communicate more coherently, affirm more generously and learn more lastingly from those around us.
>
> **(West-Burnham et al., 2007: 89)**

> Conversation is a meeting of minds with different memories and habits. When minds meet, they don't just exchange facts: they transform them, reshape them, draw different implications from them, and engage in new trains of thought. Conversation doesn't just reshuffle the cards: it creates new cards ... It's like a spark that two minds create.
>
> **(Zeldin, 1998: 14)**

Dialogue is characterised by genuine reciprocity. It is a two-way process in which there is a shared and equal commitment to respect the dignity and integrity of each of the participants. The classic form of the Socratic dialogue is the posing of a question, the identification of a problem or the expression of a disagreement. The purpose of the dialogue is to achieve a mutually acceptable resolution by the testing of alternative hypotheses, the exclusion of inappropriate arguments and fallacious conclusions and the generation of possible solutions.

There are countless ways in which the nature of dialogue might be understood, but one way in is to think in terms of different types of dialogue which have certain characteristics in common but where the context will determine the precise nature of the dialogue. Broadly, dialogue might be understood in the following ways:

→ *Personal dialogue*. This is the inner dialogue that is the basis for every other dialogue. It is the reflection, the meditation, the artistic exploration, the creative muse at work, and the personal attempts at making sense through analysing, processing and synthesising. This is the way that we internalise issues to make sense of them. Most importantly, this form of dialogue is about reflection and making meaning.

→ *Professional dialogue.* This is the discourse of work and public interaction; the discussion between doctor and doctor, the master instructing the apprentice, the academics debating, the engineers problem solving. In one sense, dialogue in this context is characterised by closed 'expert' language, a specialist vocabulary – jargon to the outsider. But this is also about public communication – the writer, the journalist and the professional communicator. This is also the language of leadership – the dialogue about values, the discourse on purpose, the questioning of technique and professional practice.

Some rules for your dialogues

The protocols for good leadership dialogue dictate that it should:

→ Be open and supportive of questioning and challenge.

→ Be respectful and inclusive.

→ Build, extend and develop each contribution.

→ Employ analytical and synthesising strategies and techniques.

→ Use regular feedback to confirm mutual comfort with content and process.

→ Focus on the problem, not the person.

→ Assume and reinforce parity of esteem between participants.

→ Promote mutual positive affirmation and reciprocity.

→ Encourage the sharing of anxieties and doubts.

→ Focus on evidence based review and planning.

→ Be accepting of silence, ambiguity and paradox.

→ Appreciate and celebrate outcomes and process.

Dialogue is most likely to be a developmental and learning process when these protocols are used to create an appropriate culture which is then open to a range of stimuli – such as this book.

Effective leadership

1   Leadership vs. management

Question

Are leadership and management different, and does it matter?

Why is this important?

One way of understanding the debate about the differences between leading and managing is to think of it in terms of a school's capacity to change. Effective management will lead to incremental improvement that is useful but may not be sufficient. Leadership, by contrast, offers the possibility of transformation.

Key quotes for the section

> The evidence suggests that many school leaders are too involved in operational and delivery matters and that this has been, to some extent, at the expense of embracing their more strategic imperatives ... But these ties to the operational space also seem to be related, based on our interpretation of the evidence, to a mindset amongst some school leaders which is often more comfortable with an operational than a strategic role.
>
> **(PricewaterhouseCoopers, 2007: 6)**

> Determined and resolute leadership from the headteacher is crucial to improving schools that require improvement. Those headteachers with a successful track record of leading schools from being judged 'satisfactory' to becoming good or better, share some common leadership characteristics. They are absolutely clear that improving teaching and learning is at the heart of what needs to be done, they communicate their high expectations of staff and pupils effectively, and they lead by example, modelling the behaviour they want from their staff. **(Ofsted, 2012: 4)**

A1

Section discussion (CD-ROM)

This is not a semantic debate. There are many nuances in the definitions of leading and managing. The debate is all-important because it provides a key indication of the relative significance attached to the two elements. The classic distinction belongs to Bennis and Nanus (1985: 21), who distinguish them in terms of leadership being about the right things and management about doing things right. Covey (1992: 101) differentiates between path making and path following. Leadership is thus defined in terms of values, vision and the future. Management is concerned with making the present work.

Which is worse – a school that is well managed and badly led or a school that is badly managed but well led? The answer is, of course, that both scenarios are potentially dysfunctional. There needs to be a balance between leadership and management that is appropriate to the school's context.

A more specific distinction might be found in the comparison between the strategic and the operational. Leadership is about the long-term vision and values of the school; management is about making the school function on a daily basis – the balance between sprint and marathon. Resource A1(i) provides a simple chart to help you to open up debate among your team, beginning by identifying your own position and viewing this in the context of the team.

Schools are complex organisations. Managing them is a sophisticated and challenging process, but that does not make it leadership. Simplistically, the strategic dimension of leadership might be understood in terms of three things: *principle* – the values informing the organisation's culture and priorities; *purpose* – the dominant view as to the *raison d'être* of the school; and *people* – the engagement, motivation and performance of people in securing the principles and purpose. Use resource A1(ii) to consider the balance your leadership team has struck over the past month of meetings. It is not necessarily desirable to have an even split in each dimension, as each school and each part of the journey will require a different focus, but this act of considering the leadership of the organisation is of great potential value for the team.

The operational aspect of leadership, by contrast, is concerned with the routines, systems, structures and procedures that translate principles and aspirations into actual practice. Leadership and management work in a symbiotic relationship, but this should always be with leadership driving management. One issue for leadership teams is to develop a vocabulary that enables effective dialogue about leading and managing. Use resource A1(iii) to analyse the minutes from your last four leadership team meetings, tally the use of the key words (or synonyms) identified and calculate the balance between leadership and management that your team are demonstrating. Are you happy with your findings? It is common for teams to find that they are focusing more time on management than on leadership. By using tools like this one, it is possible to chart your progress over time.

Key questions

What is the balance in your team between management, leadership and administration (with administration defined as work that could be done by an intelligent 16 year old, i.e. routine procedures)? How would you describe your position on this continuum? Might it be explained by the current context of the school, the expectations of staff, the prevailing school culture or a lack of debate in the school about this issue?

How do your school policies, job descriptions and performance management criteria distinguish between leading and managing? Is this distinction understood and acted on by all leaders and managers?

Do you accept the view put forward in the quotation from PricewaterhouseCoopers?

Resources (CD-ROM)

A1(i)	Finding the leadership/management balance
A1(ii)	The strategic dimension of leadership
A1(iii)	Finding the language of leadership and management

2   Moral leadership

Question

How far is your school a moral community committed to securing equity for all?

Why is this important?

Education is essentially a moral activity. Morality is a crucial factor in educating the next generation, so schools, given the nature of their professional and social responsibilities, need to be moral communities.

There also appears to be a very high correlation between schools that have a clear consensus about their values and those that achieve high performance for all.

Key quotes for the section

> The high quality and performance of Finland's educational system cannot be divorced from the clarity, characteristics of, and broad consensus about the country's broader social vision ... There is compelling clarity about and commitment to inclusive, equitable and innovative social values beyond as well as within the educational system.
>
> **(Pont et al., 2008: 80)**

> [For] the majority, the values based on the United Nations Convention on the Rights of the Child (CRC) and 'guide to life' provided by the RRSA [Rights Respecting Schools Award] has had a significant and positive influence on the school ethos, relationships, inclusivity, understanding of the wider world and the well-being of the school community, according to the adults and young people in the evaluation schools.
>
> **(Sebba and Robinson, 2010: 8)**

Section discussion (CD-ROM)

Moral leadership is often described as the challenge of converting principles into practice; abstract into concrete; the aspirational into actual experience. Moral behaviour and leadership are about behaviours that focus on complex decision making. In the final analysis, leadership is, often described as 'doing the right thing'. This immediately raises questions about what the right things are and how they are to be agreed.

Decisions imply choices, and it is in the process of choosing between options that leadership will be most clearly manifested as a higher order activity. Indeed, it could be argued that one of the most significant indicators of the transition from management to leadership, and one of the defining characteristics of highly effective school leadership, is the growth in the range and complexity of decisions that have to be taken. This implies that leaders are morally confident (i.e. they know what they believe) and that leadership teams have developed a consensus (i.e. they agree on the key principles by which they work collaboratively).

Think of a tree. Leaders have deep ethical roots – they are very clear about the fundamental principles by which they live their personal and professional lives. They convert these deeply help principles into personal values – the trunk of the tree, the basis of decision making. Finally, the branches are the day-to-day engagement with the world where ethics and values are converted into action. If the roots are shallow the tree will blow over; if the trunk is not developed the tree will not flourish; if the branches are weak they will break. Resource A2(i) represents this concept on a tree outline. Use this diagram to test the strength of your own ethical leadership.

Although there is very strong agreement about the importance of values in leadership, there is not always the same agreement about what those values should be. UNICEF identify the following core rights for every child in the UN Convention on the Rights of the Child:

→ The right to a childhood (including protection from harm).

→ The right to be educated (including all girls and boys completing primary school).

→ The right to be healthy (including having clean water, nutritious food and medical care).

→ The right to be treated fairly (which includes changing laws and practices that discriminate against children).

→ The right to be heard (which includes considering children's views).

Underpinning these principles is the principle of equity, which is perhaps best understood as all children not only having a right to go to school (equality) but also the right to go to a good school (equity). It is therefore a key function of leadership to ensure equity, consistency and fairness. Few schools would claim any issue with nailing their flag to the UNICEF mast, but many do not necessarily appreciate the full implications of this.

Use resource A2(ii) to consider the extent to which your own school walks the talk. In other words, are principles simply words to please the inspectors or are they really at the core of all you do? Answer the 10 questions by indicating where you honestly feel the school is on each issue. Once you have completed your own analysis, share this with the rest of your team. If you are unhappy that this questionnaire identifies areas where your actions do not match your words, make rectifying this a priority.

The fundamental issue for leaders and governors is whether, and the extent to which, principle informs practice. Don't assume you are a fair and equitable school just because you say so on your website!

Key questions

To what extent does principle inform practice? For example:

Are the most vulnerable children taught by the most effective teachers (e.g. members of the leadership team)?

Have banding and setting been abandoned because of the negative impact they have on most learners?

Are resources deployed to maximise the impact of intervention strategies?

Do you make maximum use of any 'spare' money?

Resources (CD-ROM)

A2(i)	The effective leadership tree
A2(ii)	The values system for your school

3   Brave leadership

Question

What part should bravery play in the role of a school leader?

Why is this important?

Education is frequently the tool by which government tries to make political and social change. Is it the role of a school leader to support the plans of a democratically elected government regardless of personal belief? Or should they fight against changes they believe are not in the best interests of pupils?

Key quotes for the section

> The opposite of bravery is not cowardice but conformity.
>
> **(Robert Anthony)**

> Neither a wise man nor a brave man lies down on the tracks of history to wait for the train of the future to run over him.
>
> **(Dwight D. Eisenhower)**

Section discussion (CD-ROM)

Are you happy with the direction in which you are being asked to take your school? Do you wake up in the morning fired up by the excitement of doing the job you trained for? If the answer to either question is no, maybe bravery is needed. However, before you attempt to repel the forthcoming inspection team by building and arming a 10 metre high barricade, bear in mind that the bravery we need may be something much more subtle. Perhaps, in this case, the bravery is *not* accepting that your only measure of success is jumping your school through the latest set of government hoops. Perhaps the bravery we are talking about here is more akin to the little boy who points out that the emperor is not actually wearing the finest set of clothes in the land, but is in danger of arrest on a public decency charge.

It is important to decide who owns the direction of travel for your school. Is it the government? Sponsors? Local authority? Governors? Leadership team? Community? Pupils? Or a balance between all of these? This is the vital first step for bravery because if you decide it isn't you, and that you have no part in the process, you have no need for courage. Simply turn up for work every day and do what you are told – and tell the emperor he looks divine. If, however, you accept part of the responsibility for the direction of your school, where do *you* think it should be going? And what makes you believe this to be the case?

Understanding your own beliefs is vital for effective leadership. Often, these will be a complex balance between your political, moral, religious and personal views, and the experiences you have gained as a school leader or classroom practitioner. You will probably also have ideas and opinions from observed practice and research. This will all be mixed together into a complex stew, often referred to as 'gut'. This gut feeling, once properly investigated and substantiated, should not be discarded but actually used as your touchstone for the journey ahead. Too often, leaders are so focused on the next step in the path that they fail to notice the journey they are on. They accept that some greater force is guiding their way and that completion of the day's tasks is all that is needed to succeed. Challenge the journey you are on as a team. Spend time deciding if the current direction of travel is in agreement with the aims you share for the school.

Use resource A3(i) to focus your discussion about what constituent parts your school is aiming for. Are all the arrows pointing in the same way? If you wish to investigate this in more detail, use the arrow template to reproduce the diagram on a larger scale, using one arrow for each group. This may help you to decide where your priorities should lie – any arrow that is clearly aiming in a different direction should not be ignored.

Resource A3(ii) will help you to focus on what you are currently doing and how this fits into the overall direction of your school. Are you currently on a carefully charted journey or a series of random meanderings?

Now is the time for courage. Bravery without direction is pointless and very foolhardy; bravery must be associated with clarity of thinking and an ability to explain that vision widely. It could be argued that fearlessness should be a skill that is internally awarded rather than acknowledged by others. In other words, if someone remarks, 'Isn't she/he a brave leader?', might this be because they are perceived as going where others would not? Maybe true bravery is giving colleagues the self-belief that the path to be travelled is the one they wish to embark on.

The brave leadership team is many times more powerful than a brave head. A leadership team that deliberately chooses a daring path will do so having considered the risks and understood the difficulties the journey ahead may hold. Use resource A3(iii) to focus the team on finding a clear consensus on the next stage for the school. Distilling the complexity of a school into this simple diagram could be one of the most effective things you could do to move your school forwards. Can you all agree over what your school is about? Why it exists? And how you will know that it is successful? If your team is motivated by this new clarity of purpose, a team bravery pledge is included for signing (A3(iv))!

Key questions

Who is setting the direction in your school? What is it?

Do you fully agree with the direction of travel?

How have your own opinions been formed? Do they stand up to scrutiny?

When did you last share your vision for the school?

How can you show brave leadership to get there?

Are you part of a brave leadership team?

Resources (CD-ROM)

A3(i)	Who leads your school?
A3(ii)	Do your views stand up to scrutiny?
A3(iii)	What is the direction for your school?
A3(iv)	Bravery pledge

A4

4 Leadership learning and development

Question

How do we develop and sustain highly effective leaders?

Why is this important?

There is a direct and very clear correlation between the quality of leadership and the potential capacity of a school to improve. One of the most powerful strategies available to a school is to invest in developing its own leaders.

Key quotes for the section

> A large number of quantitative studies in North America ... show that school leadership influences performance more than any other variable except socio-economic background and the quality of teaching. **(Barber et al., 2010: 5)**

> The crux of leadership development that works is *self-directed learning*: intentionally developing or strengthening an aspect of who you are or who you want to be, or both. This requires first getting a strong image of your *ideal self*, as well as an accurate picture of your *real self* – who you are now. Such self-directed learning is most effective and sustainable when you understand the process of change – and the steps to achieve it as you go through it. The kind of learning is recursive: the steps do not unfold in a smooth, orderly way, but rather follow a sequence, with each step demanding different amounts of time and effort. **(Goleman et al., 2002: 109)**

Section discussion (CD-ROM)

Investing in leadership development is one of the main components of any strategy to secure improvement, improve teaching and learning and embed sustainable change. Leadership development seems to be most likely to make an impact on the quality of teaching and learning and the development of sustainable high performance if it focuses on the following principles:

→ *Learning for understanding rather than the transmission of information (training) or engagement with abstract theory.* Learning for understanding involves developing the confidence to apply and act through certain key behaviours.

→ *Coaching and mentoring.* The one-to-one seems to have the greatest potential to translate theory into consistent and effective practice.

→ *Experiential learning (learning to lead by actually leading).* The use of real-time genuine leadership projects, internships, job swaps and other similar activities seem to have the best impact in terms of confidence and the ability to act with confidence.

→ *Collaborative learning projects.* These have significant potential for accelerating leadership learning within the team, between teams and across the school, as well as developing confidence in working in different environments.

Use resource A4(i) to investigate the leadership development of the team you work in. Ask everyone to identify key experiences which have been used to develop their leadership. Attempt to categorise them under the headings provided. If there is not a balance of strategies, focus on how the team can address this.

Two major learning processes seem to be central to leadership development. First, there is a need for challenge. Learning activities need to be challenging and facilitators needs to be challenging in order to encourage deep engagement with the learning process. The second element is reflection. There is very powerful evidence that successful professionals are highly reflective about their work. This is where coaches and mentors can play a significant role, but leadership development means that individuals become reflective in every aspect of their work and are comfortable and confident in reviewing their practice. Resource A4(ii) encourages internal reflection to consider your strengths and needs in the areas of reflection and challenge. Discuss your review with others in your team.

All of these approaches assume an underpinning of knowledge of the theory and practice of school leadership. This implies a working knowledge of, for example, research into the most effective uses of the Pupil Premium, the current research on classroom practice and the evidence base for high impact leadership of teaching and learning. One very practical example of how research can inform leadership practice is the regular sharing of reading in leadership team meetings – that is, actually putting reading and discussion on the agenda. A copy of resource A4(iii) would make a very positive addition to the minutes of any leadership team. Encourage regular updates and circulate among the whole staff. An online version of the chart could contain hyperlinks to the actual work.

As is clear from the introduction to this book, all of these strategies are essentially the warp of leadership development – the weft is dialogue. Fundamental to every leadership development activity and, more importantly, fundamental to the daily routines of every leader, is a commitment to engaging in learning conversations with other leaders, colleagues, pupils and their parents.

Key questions

To what extent is leadership development embedded into the school structure and processes? Are there strategies to support middle leaders, aspiring senior leaders, classroom leaders, pupils and governors?

Who is responsible for succession planning and leadership development in your school?

What provision is available in the school, across the teaching school alliance, the trust or federation?

What does the monitoring and evaluation of leadership development in your school tell you about the most cost effective strategies?

How deeply embedded is a culture of coaching and mentoring in your school?

Resources (CD-ROM)

A4(i)	Leadership development in your team
A4(ii)	Personal strengths and weaknesses
A4(iii)	Record of research reading

5   Creating school cultures

Question

Is school culture constructed, or is it simply the product of its activities? Is it wise for a leadership team to try to define the culture?

Why is this important?

If a school's culture influences its effectiveness, surely it would be wise for the leadership team to, first, be able to describe its culture and then, more importantly, make alterations to it.

Key quotes for the section

> Culture is intangible, but it's essential: you can walk into a school and know immediately whether you want to be there or not. The same thing goes for the students, and the staff.
>
> **(Haberman, 2013)**

> There is a long-standing controversy about the relationship between culture and leadership. Do leaders shape culture or are they shaped by it? Is symbolic leadership empowering or manipulative? Another debate swirls around the link between culture and results. Do organizations with robust cultures outperform those relying on structure and strategy?
>
> **(Bolman and Deal, 2013: 264)**

Section discussion (CD-ROM)

'Our school supports the individual and nurtures talent', claims the sign across the door of Maydup Academy. Is this the school culture? At what point does our optimism diminish? Is it when we wander through the door to take a wobbly, chewing gum embossed seat in reception, to witness a red faced teacher exchanging syllables with a hollow eyed pupil from a saliva dripping breath away? Or when the office informs us that staff absence is at an all time high? Or when a dishevelled supply teacher barges past muttering that he will never, ever darken the door again? If we take school culture to encompass the attitudes, behaviour and ethos of the school, this surely must be something that is best measured by a multitude of views and from a range of viewpoints. While the leader may be the person most easily able to alter the culture of a school, might it be possible that they are, in fact, one of the least able to reliably measure it? If the leadership team are keen to obtain a true grasp on the matter a concerted effort is vital. To aid in analysing a school's culture, it is helpful to have an understanding of the three most commonly identified descriptors used: bureaucratic, collegial and toxic.

→ *Bureaucratic*. In these schools there is a clear boss at the front and a real focus on things being done in a set way. This is a rules driven organisation, with little focus on the interactions between peers. Teachers are expected to reach a set standard but are not encouraged to develop beyond that. Discipline problems are often seen as the student's problem, and teachers are expected to develop their own solutions.

→ *Collegial*. These are schools which prioritise experimentation and high expectations. There is a reliance on mutual trust and honesty at all levels of the organisation as well as strong support systems. Leaders will make it evident that answers do not lie with individuals but within networks. Rewards are a key component, often built into the day-to-day life of the school, many interlaced with humour. Staff (at all levels) and pupils are encouraged to be part of the decision making process, but there is usually clear protection for the most important values. There is often a focus on tradition and ceremony – the building of a 'family'.

→ *Toxic*. Students are regarded as a problem in these schools. Many parts of the organisation are hostile towards change and believe they are already doing the best they can. Staffroom chatter is frequently negative and the stories told are often lowering and demoralising. Staff rarely share ideas, materials or solutions, as they tend to mistrust new ideas. Individuals focus on failure, whether that is the pupils, staff or leaders. There is little celebration of success, either formal or informal.

Here are some tools to begin measuring the culture in your school:
→ School culture questionnaire: pupil – A5(i)
→ School culture questionnaire: staff – A5(ii)
→ School culture questionnaire: visitor – A5(iii)
→ School culture questionnaire: leader – A5(iv)

Arrange for these surveys to be completed on a regular basis. Use the information you gather to define the percentage of each type of culture within your school. Are you happy with the results? If you are content with your findings then it is important to consider what methods you can employ to ensure this remains the case. This exercise should be carried out at least twice a year to check that you are still on track. However, if your team is uncomfortable with the findings then use the monitoring resource (A5(v)) to identify areas for improvement, and then repeat the process after a defined interval to measure progress. Ensure that there is good attention to detail. Changing the culture of a school is not an instantaneous matter. Deciding that a change is needed is only the first step, but it is a vital one.

Key questions

Can you define your school in terms of a bureaucratic, collegial or toxic culture?

Is this what your leadership team is happy with?

What are the main barriers to the culture being changed?

What would be the benefits of moving towards an improved culture? Would they make the effort to change worthwhile?

How can your team accelerate any change needed?

Resources (CD-ROM)

A5(i)	School culture questionnaire: pupil
A5(ii)	School culture questionnaire: staff
A5(iii)	School culture questionnaire: visitor
A5(iv)	School culture questionnaire: leader
A5(v)	School culture summary sheet

A6

6 Accountability

Question

What type of accountability systems are appropriate for school leaders?

Why is this important?

All countries expect some measure of accountability from their school leaders, although the type and depth of accountability vary greatly. It is important for a leader to understand the accountability systems under which they operate and work out their own role within it.

Key quotes for the section

> We believe that public services will improve most when professionals feel free to do what they believe is right, and are properly accountable for the results. Schools should evidently be accountable for achieving a minimum level of performance because taxpayers have a right to expect that their money will be used effectively to educate pupils and equip them to take their place in society. But in recent years schools have suffered from a compliance regime that drove them to meet a bewildering array of centrally-imposed government targets. Schools should, instead, be accountable to parents, pupils and communities for how well they perform.
>
> **(DfE, 2010: 66)**

> ASCL embraces the importance of accountability, welcomes reduction in bureaucracy and supports a cohesive and fair national education system for all. ASCL believes that accountability is most effective for all partners in the education service when there is a climate of mutual trust and respect, which is a feature of many of the high performing education systems globally, where schools and teachers are held in high esteem and there is national consensus about the importance of high achievement for all. This should involve schools in holding themselves to account through ever more focused self-evaluation.
>
> **(ASCL, 2012: 2)**

Section discussion (CD-ROM)

Accountability is fundamental to any relationship where an individual or organisation provides a service on behalf of another individual or organisation. Accountability is usually seen as a demonstration that the service or product required has been supplied in accordance with three possible outcomes:

1 According to identified standards and to demonstrate compliance (regulatory accountability).

2 To demonstrate the achievement of a range of outcomes or performance criteria (market accountability).

3 To show adherence to moral and professional standards (professional accountability).

Use resource A6(i) to analyse your own strands of accountability. Allocate the accountabilities you encounter to the appropriate sector, and for each one indicate the strength of the influence on your practice.

Accountability systems usually operate hierarchically – that is, holding subordinates to account is one of the key functions of leaders in hierarchical and bureaucratic systems. Indeed, the pattern of accountability often determines the structure of an organisation. What seems to be more important, however, is that all models of accountability are based on objective judgements grounded in valid evidence; the process is transparent and the criteria are public and agreed. Think of the work of your own team – would you classify your own systems as bureaucratic or transparent and evidence based?

There are virtually no education systems that have no model of accountability. Most work through professional accountability, many through market based approaches (e.g. parents) and some through regulatory accountability. England is probably one of the very few countries that operates all three models (lucky us!). Finland, by contrast, seems to function almost completely on professional accountability based on trust.

For school leaders in England, regulatory accountability is manifested in the Ofsted inspection process – the process whereby judgements are made against public criteria according to the extent to which a school is meeting appropriate levels of performance. School reports and league tables drive market accountability, largely focused on supporting parental choice of school.

For many English schools, professional standards published by the Department for Education serve as the basis for performance management and may therefore have an element of the regulatory about them. *The Teachers' Standards* are reproduced in A6(ii). Look at these with a critical eye. Do you monitor these standards in an open and evidence based way? Do teachers in your school see these as a useful guide or as a stick with which they can be beaten?

A6

A major issue when it comes to holding a professional to account is the extent to which that individual is able to manage the variables that might impact on their performance. It would seem to go against the principles of natural justice to hold somebody accountable for something over which they have no control. This situation has led to calls for 'intelligent accountability' which might have the characteristics identified in the previous quotation from the ASCL policy paper.

A further concern is that the pressures of regulatory and market based accountability might compromise professional accountability. In Finland, it is the teachers' union that publishes the moral code, part of which is reproduced in A6(iii). Analyse the work of your own team against this code. Do you feel your work measures up? Use the table to consider your accountability systems under the headings of human worth, honesty and teachers' relationship to work. It is important not just to blindly accept the accountability framework you inherit but to engage fully with it. Ensure that your leadership does not let the system become soulless and instead develop it into a vibrant support to help the improvement of your school.

Key questions

What types of accountability do you face?

Do you use professional standards in a supportive or bureaucratic way?

How does your school compare to the Finnish accountability framework?

Are you using accountability to measure rather than to grow?

Resources (CD-ROM)

A6(i)	How accountable are you?
A6(ii)	The Teachers' Standards
A6(iii)	How does your school measure up against the Finnish accountability system?

Thinking strategically

1   From improvement to transformation

Question

Is improvement enough?

Why is this important?

If education is to meet the demands of a new society, can this be done through an approach focused on incremental improvement, or is transformation required?

Key quotes for the section

> Transformation literally means going beyond your form.
>
> **(Wayne Dyer)**

> If you always do what you have always done then you will always get what you always got.
>
> **(Attributed variously to Mark Twain, Henry Ford and Bill Clinton)**

> [T]ransformation attacks both the current and the known world and the future. It is concerned with the creation of new opportunities, with the ability to junk conventional wisdom and destroy old (often cherished) advantages, to violate established business practice, compete in different ways, shut down competitors' angle of attack and behave in counterintuitive and, indeed, unpredictable ways.
>
> **(Taffinder, 1998: 36)**

> We cannot restructure a structure that is splintered at its roots. Adding wings to caterpillars does not create butterflies – it creates awkward and dysfunctional caterpillars. Butterflies are created through transformation.
>
> **(Marshall, 1995: 1)**

Section discussion (CD-ROM)

The world is changing … fast. The needs of society are changing … fast. The needs of pupils are changing … fast. Education is changing … but is it fast enough?

Politicians, the media and many within the system itself are calling for a change in our education system, but often the changes that occur are incremental rather than transformational. Clearly, year-on-year improvement can produce notable change, but frequently there seems to be a limit to the progress made. Even Sir Dave Brailsford's much quoted 'marginal gains' approach for the Sky cycling team (improving many factors by a small increment) has shown its limits when other teams deploy novel materials or radical new training systems.

Think of the successful video shop owner in the 1990s who sank all his profits into improving the number of VHS titles available for loan, but failed to notice that changing to a digital format would be his route to success. Are we in danger of continuing to focus on improving a VHS education system when a digital system is what is required?

Assuming that your leadership team is not blessed with a clairvoyant (we hear Mystic Meg is looking for a new opening), information on the challenges ahead must be limited to the process of scenario planning – that is, considering what options might arise from alternative actions now. Approached positively this can be extremely valuable and should certainly not be a soft option, left until the infinite list of management tasks are completed.

Use resource B1(i) as the focus for planning around teaching and learning in your school. Make an honest (warts and all) appraisal of your current situation. Identify the things you wouldn't want a visitor to see – the things you are least proud of. For example, are there teachers you avoid showing in action? If so, what effect does 'learning' in their classroom have on the pupils who experience their brand of teaching every day (the pupils who do not share your luxury of avoidance)?

Initially, take a 'marginal gains' approach: investigate five things you could improve and consider how each could be improved by 5%. Does this bring about the type of change you need? For example, if teachers develop quicker registration techniques, homework recording systems or if punctuality between lessons is improved, would the extra minutes gained be used effectively to deepen learning? (Five extra 'learning' minutes each lesson would produce 83 hours of additional learning space!)

Does the 5% approach help you to develop the school and to produce young people ready to make the most of 2050? If so, for now, concentrate on the improvements, but be aware that Handy's (1994) work on the sigmoid curve warns that long term progress requires transformative action at crucial junctures. Resource B1(iii) shows you what this model looks like. The key point of the sigmoid curve model is that leaders have a responsibility to explore transformative change while things are apparently going well. To many this will seem counterintuitive – why change when things are improving? In response, it is only necessary to mention certain football teams (whatever happened to Accrington Stanley?). Or consider the city of Detroit. In the 1960s it was the economic powerhouse of the USA; by 2010 its population had fallen by 60% from its all-time high. The city was in economic decline with massive unemployment, abandoned homes and factories and seemingly light years away from the glory days of Motown. The message is very simple: *Sic transit gloria mundi*! Better to prevent collapse than to try to recover.

If you feel that you require more than a marginal gains approach, consider three possible transformations that could dramatically improve the long term trajectory of the school. Use resource B1(ii) to structure your ideas. Do not simply consider tweaks to existing practice; instead, try to find new ways of solving the problem, even if some appear ludicrous or unrealistic. (If they are ludicrously unrealistic, you will have plenty of opportunity to get rid of them later.) For each develop a scenario. Discuss the possible benefits and drawbacks. In the initial discussion, do not over-focus on practicalities – many transformative ideas are dismissed long before their true potential is recognised. If sufficient members of the leadership team are interested in a proposed trans-formation, appoint champions whose role it is to investigate the feasibility more broadly across the school.

The only thing worse than not looking to transform lives is to have the idea but to do nothing about it!

Key questions

What is in need of improvement in your school?

How could each area be improved by 5%?

B1

If this was achieved, would you be content?

Do you need to consider radical alternatives?

What could you do that would transform how your pupils approach learning?

Resources (CD-ROM)

B1(i)	Improve or transform?
B1(ii)	Possible transformations
B1(iii)	Sigmoid curve

2   Leading through vision

Question

Do you have a vision for the school that is known, shared, understood and acted on?

Why is this important?

The potential for any organisation to succeed is significantly influenced by the extent to which it has a sense of shared identity and common purpose.

Key quotes for the section

> Vision, if it is to be ethical and effective in dealing with a highly complex, potentially democratic world needs to be informed by the variety of voices trying to make sense of their individual and collective lives ... articulation of a vision is still important for a new type of passionate leader. Being able to put possibilities into words is an important skill ... imagination, as John Dewey noted, is the chief instrument of the good.
>
> **(Novak, 2008: 40)**

> The three things that most make people happy are purposes, power and relationships. Teachers feel positive emotions when their purposes are clear, focused and achievable, and when the purposes belong to them. They become unhappy when purposes are vague, scattered, unrealistic, constantly changing, or are imposed by someone else.
>
> **(Hargreaves and Shirley, 2009: 73)**

Section discussion (CD-ROM)

There is a very strong case for arguing that leaders are at their most effective when they are working with their colleagues to secure a shared vision. However, there is nothing less effective than a vision that is the private property of the leader – that is the basis for a dictatorship. A vision is only a vision to the extent that it is known, shared, understood and acted on. The role of leaders is to initiate the process of establishing a shared vision, not to announce that vision or to impose it, but to enable and facilitate the emergence of consensus and shared commitment.

Use resource B2(i) to consider the extent to which the leader's vision is understood and shared in your own organisation. Avoid searching out staff who are 'on message' – the more people you ask, the more secure you can be in your findings.

A school's vision is essentially a statement that encapsulates its core values and beliefs: its sense of purpose, the outcomes it is working towards and, perhaps most importantly, a sense of the importance and significance of the school's work. A vision should be exciting, challenging, motivating, aspirational and possible. At its very best a vision has the potential to:

→ Develop a shared sense of purpose and mission.

→ Build a common language.

→ Inform, prioritise and focus performance and outcomes.

→ Serve to motivate, engage and secure commitment.

→ Define and clarify the nature of work.

A school's vision needs to include a number of key elements:

→ A commitment to core values.

→ An explicit statement of purpose – the business we are in.

→ A clear sense of priorities.

→ An indication of how the school will be if the vision is translated into practice.

Use resource B2(ii) to examine your own vision. Does it embody these elements? For these elements to be realised, the vision has to be embedded in every aspect of school life (e.g. all policies, strategic and improvement planning, the budget, monitoring and evaluation, job descriptions, every aspect of the pupil experience, the school's relationships). In essence, a school's values should be like a stick of rock – it does not matter where it is broken, the message is consistent throughout.

Leaders are at their most effective when they see translating the values of the school into actual practice as a vital component of their work. They can do this by:

→ Engaging all members of the school community in dialogue around the vision.

→ Modelling the vision in practical ways.

→ Monitoring and reviewing the extent to which the vision is central to the work of every member of the school community.

All of these points depend on two basic assumptions: first, that all leaders share and accept the vision and, second, that it is a living part of their daily working life. Develop a strategy for a more cohesive implementation of your vision – B2(iii) offers a template for supporting this.

Key questions

To what extent are you confident that your vision is known, shared, accepted and acted on by every member of the school community?

Is your vision fit for purpose? Is it up to date, and does it reflect the changing policy context of education and the needs of our community?

Do all leaders and governors work to implement the vision in a consistent way?

Resources (CD-ROM)

B2(i)	How well is your vision shared?
B2(ii)	Checking your vision
B2(iii)	Whole school implementation

B3

3 Developing future scenarios

Question

Are you preparing pupils for a range of possible futures by developing alternative scenarios for their education?

Why is this important?

If a core purpose of education is helping young people to become effective citizens, it is important to realise that the future needs of these young citizens may be very different to those presently required.

Key quotes for the section

> The route ahead is never a nice, straight line. One of many alternative futures will emerge.
>
> **(Woody Wade)**

> Decision makers can use scenarios to think about the uncertain aspects of the future that most worry them, to discover the aspects about which they should be concerned, and to explore ways in which these might unfold.
>
> **(Shell, 2008: CS5)**

Section discussion (CD-ROM)

Will tomorrow be similar to today? How about the day after? And the one after that? We all know that with each day that passes more variability is introduced, with more opportunity for chance to intervene, and the process of forecasting becomes increasingly problematic. If school leadership uses this form of future forecasting it is very unlikely that it will be able to respond to any of the surprises awaiting society. Prediction that is based on a mathematical approach (the assumption that change occurs in an incremental fashion) is fraught with difficulty. The shop owner who predicted his future needs solely on a spreadsheet study of trends may not have foreseen the complete change in shopping habits caused by the advent of online retail. The customers still require goods, but finding new ways of meeting those needs is essential to long term success.

Similarly, the school that assumes its only concern should be to increase the percentage of pupils achieving exam success every year may be floored in a future world that focuses on pupil creativity and attitude. Scenario planning is a technique now used widely across business, academia and, increasingly, the public sector. Scenario planning does not take an incremental approach to the current situation, but looks to imagine a range of alternative futures. If you consider the needs of your pupils for several different visions, there is a greatly improved chance that you will be versatile enough to support them whatever changes occur in our society.

Scenarios are essentially descriptions of a preferred future – where we would like to be. We all use scenarios in every aspect of our lives. A child might switch between being a racing driver, a nurse and an explorer, once working with animals has been excluded. Couples will explore the possibilities of their lives together by speculating about their future options. People approaching the end of their working lives will begin to investigate the options for retirement. Middle leaders will often have ambitions for their professional futures that are best seen as possible scenarios.

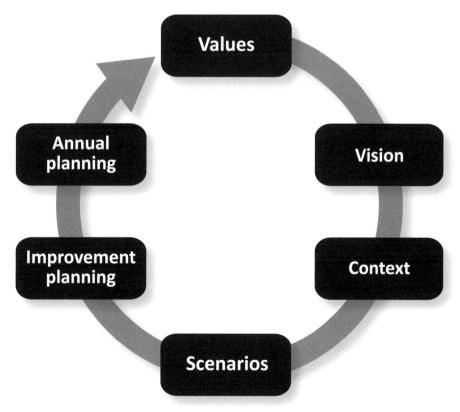

The components of scenario planning

B3

Scenarios are the product of three elements: the values that are fundamental to the school; the vision, expressed through the hopes and fears that we have for the school in the future; and a pragmatic awareness of the history of the school, the prevailing policy context and the constraints limiting the school's potential development.

The greater the time span you consider, the greater the range of extremes. Primary schools are faced with an even bigger dilemma – the scenarios for your future citizens may be 12 years away. Scenario planning at this length has a greater element of chance built in, and may be deemed less relevant unless completed alongside the secondary schools in the area. Clearly, producing random, guideless scenarios would be very time consuming and has the potential to waste the energy of your team. Instead, consider producing responses to the following range of possibilities over a five year time span.

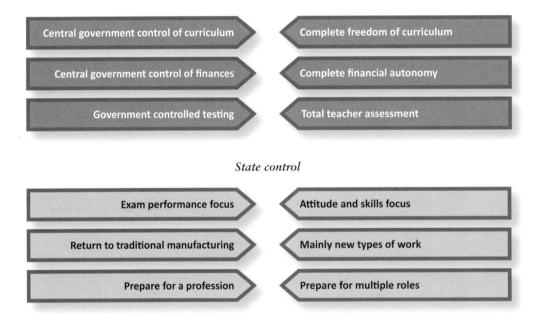

Central government control of curriculum	Complete freedom of curriculum
Central government control of finances	Complete financial autonomy
Government controlled testing	Total teacher assessment

State control

Exam performance focus	Attitude and skills focus
Return to traditional manufacturing	Mainly new types of work
Prepare for a profession	Prepare for multiple roles

Possible scenarios for pupils on leaving school

Each of these is an extreme, and the reality five years from now is likely to be some way away from them. It is equally unlikely that there will be perfect balance between the two. Considering your team's approach to the various scenarios will help to improve your current practice and ensure that you are not simply focused on the next steps ahead. Complete resources B3(i–vi) to begin your work.

It is all too obvious that the world is not rational, predictable or controllable, so why do we persist in vain attempts to plan our futures in detail? Scenarios are possible, preferred futures that inform short term improvement planning. In the same way, very few couples have a strategic plan for their lives together – there are just too many complex variables at work. However, this does not preclude conversations about their preferred future together and taking appropriate steps towards translating aspirations into reality.

Key questions

What assumptions are you currently making that may be wrong?

What time period are you happy scenario planning for?

What area of scenario planning do you think would be most useful for your school?

How well prepared would you be for any scenario?

What changes are you going to make to your current practice in light of your findings?

Resources (CD-ROM)

B3(i)	Scenario planning: control
B3(ii)	Scenario planning: finances
B3(iii)	Scenario planning: testing
B3(iv)	Scenario planning (pupil needs): exams
B3(v)	Scenario planning (pupil needs): careers
B3(vi)	Scenario planning (pupil needs): professions

B4

4   Exploring alternative futures

Question

Are schools fit for purpose? Given all the social changes that are taking place, do we need to radically rethink schools and schooling?

Why is this important?

Schools exist to serve the needs of society. However, they are also fundamental in creating a future society. Many aspects of our public services have changed in recent years, but schools seem to be remarkably resilient in resisting transformation. Change in education tends to be incremental, but is it time to question the status quo and rethink the basic assumptions under which schools are working?

Key quotes for the section

> Educational systems are inherently conservative institutions, and that conservatism is in many ways justified. Still, just as educational systems eventually adapted to the agricultural and industrial revolutions, just as they eventually responded to the decline of established religion and the invention of print and audio visual technologies, they will have to adapt as well to the facts of the globalized, knowledge-centred economy and society.
>
> **(Gardner, 2006: 225)**

> The world our children are living in is changing four times faster than our schools.
>
> **(William Daggett)**

Section discussion (CD-ROM)

In most important aspects, education in England, and almost every other major education system, has hardly changed for over 100 years. The architecture of schools (buildings etc.), the deployment of time (terms and the school day), the nature of pedagogy and the content of the curriculum are fundamentally the same. True, there have been significant shifts of emphasis, but the core assumptions underpinning schools are substantially the same as they were in the 19th century.

There are a number of factors that now point to the need to question prevailing orthodoxies in many education systems. For example:

→ The lack of equity and limited inclusion across the system.

→ The failure to engage with the impact of social and economic factors on education.

→ The changing nature of employment and employability.

→ The impact of information technology.

→ The implications of continuing social change.

→ The potential impact of continuing climate change.

Consider how the nature of personal transport, travel and communication has been transformed. How would medical practice be now if it had only changed to the same extent that education has?

In education, there are a number of areas that might be seen as offering the potential for significant change and realignment, with schools acting on their own initiative rather than being directed by government policy:

→ Focusing on social, physical and emotional well-being as the precursor to securing equity.

→ Engaging with families and communities by seeing them as partners in education.

→ Developing schools as community resources.

→ Seeing employability as a valid educational outcome for all.

→ Realigning teaching and learning around information technology.

→ Developing collaborative relationships with other schools, social agencies and businesses.

→ Schools leading social enterprise to recognise social and environmental issues.

Take a stock check – how are things moving in your own school? Resource B4(i) will help you to look at how you are responding to the issues above.

In many communities, schools are the most significant social resource and, potentially, powerful agents for change and innovation. The danger is that schools become living fossils, reflecting a view of learning and education that is only valid and relevant in the internal worlds of education. Develop a 'what if?' approach to change management. What if the school continues to work unchanged over 50 years? What if the school had never existed? Resource B4(ii) will help your team to explore a number of 'what if?' questions, but please develop your own as well. This is not just a game, but can be the start of some very serious discussions about how your school could transform. Don't let the conversation stop here – make sure that you widen the discussion around your school.

This process, in essence moving from incremental improvement to transformational thinking, is very much what leadership needs to become if schools are to avoid becoming increasingly irrelevant. This will require leaders who are comfortable and confident in challenging deeply help assumptions, who are open to alternative perspectives and innovation, and who are willing to change their own approaches and behaviours.

Key questions

Why does the teaching profession continue to reify the position of head teacher?

Why are most schools closed for over 80% of the year?

Why don't schools focus on well-being as the essential precursor to successful learning?

Why is the totally artificial process of transfer from primary to secondary at the age of 11 still the norm?

Why are many schools still an island 'entire of itself'?

Why are schools designed around the curriculum rather than learning?

Resources (CD-ROM)

B4(i)	How well is your school responding to change?
B4(ii)	What if ...?

5   Spiral thinking

Question

Does life occur in straight lines or in spirals?

Why is this important?

If we are to be effective leaders, we need to ensure that our thinking is aligned to the way in which things change and not to the way in which we think they change.

Key quotes for the section

> The spiral in a snail's shell is the same mathematically as the spiral in the Milky Way galaxy, and it's also the same mathematically as the spirals in our DNA. It's the same ratio that you'll find in very basic music that transcends cultures all over the world.
>
> **(Joseph Gordon-Levitt)**

> This process, thinking spirally, is at the heart of knowledge work. Knowledge work is the work of producing new ideas, solutions and ways of thinking about problems – old and new. Knowledge work involves solving problems and completing projects. It is more than simply gathering information ... Spiral development is collaborative in nature and requires a high level of interaction among the members of a community.
>
> **(Megill, 2013: 114)**

Section discussion (CD-ROM)

As leaders, we want to prepare our organisation for the complexities that lie ahead. How do we do this? Often, our default position is to assume that the current trajectory of travel is the one that will always be, that like a ball travelling through the air our thinking should follow a set of rules. This thinking does not prepare us for the surprises that may lie ahead – the gust of wind or even the impending obstacle.

From the times of our early ancestors, humans have had a tendency to shape life into straight lines and boxes. The desire for simplicity has led us to assume that life is linear, when in fact DNA, the very building block of life, is a complex helix. Spiral based structures are common in nature and may make a better model for our thinking process.

B5

Spiralling out

If you have an idea that you would like to expand, instead of tabulating it, approach its development in a spiral way. For example, consider the modern curriculum. Many parts of it are presented as a learning ladder, a series of facts which are assumed to build on each other, and the students progress through it in a linear way and at a constant rate. The notion that learning occurs in steps is built into its very fabric, yet few of us really believe that this is an effective way to consider it. When parents help their infant to acquire 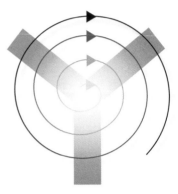 language, for example, they naturally use a spiral approach of repetition, gradually expanding their child's learning.

Imagine you are responsible for the complete learning of a child from birth until adulthood (which, between all our readers, we are!). Wouldn't a spiral model be more appropriate than a linear one? Our current planning allows for a pupil to completely miss an essential 'never to be repeated' nugget of information ('Sorry Officer, I had the flu when they did drugs education'). Consider the system of education common in rural communities 100 years ago – the one room school. A child would experience a similar diet of topics each year, but would develop their understanding of the subject each time they met it. As they grew older, they would participate in deeper learning while also helping to introduce the topic to their younger class mates. Each journey around the spiral allows the individual to make sense of the learning and place it in a context, rather than view it as a series of disconnected facts.

Could a spiralling out approach be used to improve the curriculum across your school or in specific subject areas? Resource B5(i) can be used as a template for developing your own spiralling out thinking as a leader. Choose three themes for your focus and consider how these would develop each time you meet them on your journey out of the spiral. For example, if you would like to improve your homework policy, start with why you want a policy and then spiral out your thinking, perhaps using pupil understanding, pupil motivation and parental engagement as your three foci.

Spiralling in

When spiralling in, the spiral generates future possibilities and helps you to broaden your long term planning. If the process is considered in reverse, it can be used to help you to bring clarity to your decision making. Broader desires/wishes are taken on

board and the implementation strategy is then considered in the light of the effect this will have on various areas of the organisation.

Focus on a decision you wish to make. Decide on three areas that might be influenced by your decision and for each one consider the potential outcomes/effects as you spiral towards your decision. Resource B5(ii) will help your process. For example, you might want to introduce a new performance management system for your staff. Start your spiral and consider the effect it has on three areas: staff skills, staff morale and pupil progress. Each time the spiral crosses a box, consider how the area effects the development of your system.

Key questions

What problems do you wish to solve?

Does a linear solution seem likely for this problem?

Are you trying to come to a single precise decision? (If so, spiral in.)

Are you trying to develop an effective long term strategy? (If so, spiral out.)

What actions will be made as a result of this work?

Resources (CD-ROM)

| B5(i) | Spiralling out |
| B5(ii) | Spiralling in |

Leading innovation and change

1   Leading through creativity

Question

How far would you characterise your school as being committed to developing a culture of creativity?

Why is this important?

Every school faces challenges in terms of a combination of issues relating to securing excellence and equity for all and/or developing an educational experience fit for life in the 21st century. Simply continuing to replicate historic approaches may well not solve these problems, and nor will exhortations to work harder. For many of the issues facing schools, a totally new approach is necessary in order to ensure that they are able to respond to the short term challenges of changing government policy and the long term challenges of rethinking schools and schooling.

Key quotes for the section

> The things we fear most in organizations – fluctuations, disturbances, imbalances – are the primary sources of creativity.
>
> **(Margaret Wheatley)**

> Creativity requires the courage to let go of certainty.
>
> **(Attributed to Erich Fromm)**

> You can never solve a problem using the thinking that created it.
>
> **(Attributed to Albert Einstein)**

C1

> An effective leader needs creative skills and attitudes to generate powerful ideas; analytical intelligence to determine whether they are good ideas; practical intelligence to implement the ideas effectively and to persuade others to listen to and follow the ideas; and wisdom to ensure that the ideas represent a common good.
>
> **(Sternberg, 2005: 348)**

> If you're not prepared to be wrong, you'll never come up with something original.
>
> **(Robinson, 2006)**

Section discussion (CD-ROM)

Creativity is about great art and music and literature. It is also about technological innovation and scientific research and, increasingly, it is being seen as a facet of effective leadership. If leadership is about translating principle into practice, 'doing the right thing' and creating the future, then it has to be about creativity. Not necessarily the polymath creativity of a Leonardo or an individual genius but rather working with others to find better ways of doing important things.

David Perkins has developed the 'snowflake model of creativity' – that is, six psychological elements, each complex in its own right and interacting in a highly complex way. According to Perkins (1981), the more of these traits a person has, the more creative they tend to be. The six traits may be defined as:

1   The need to structure and clarify that which is seemingly chaotic. Creative people have a high tolerance for complexity and ambiguity; they thrive on synthesising and making sense.

2   The ability to identify problems and then understand the components of the problem (i.e. asking the right questions and then exploring a wide range of options to find answers).

3   The skills and strategies to find new perspectives and different approaches. For example, thinking in opposites and contraries and challenging assumptions.

4   The willingness to take risks, to seek challenges and an associated acceptance of the possibility of failure. The ability to learn from failure as a means of pursuing personal boundaries and competence.

5   The willingness to be open to criticism, to take feedback and to test ideas against the perceptions of others.

6   Creative people are intrinsically motivated; they relish challenge and derive enjoyment from the work itself. Intrinsic motivation is about the joy and passion of the creative process; it is not about rewards, recognition or status.

Use resource C1(i) to look at the creativity within your leadership group. The simple snowflake should be the focus for considering the strengths and weaknesses within your group. Remember, this is about measuring your creativity – you don't have to stay within the lines! Use colour to highlight your successes and your challenges in each of the six areas.

Then use resource C1(ii) to chart how you can support creativity within your team to ensure that your school is best served for the next few years. We provide the blank with no other stipulation than that this should be completed creatively, and that once it is produced it should not sit in a drawer gathering chewing gum but be used as a regular reminder of the path ahead.

It is clear from these six characteristics that creativity is as much an emotional as a cognitive process. It is a complex blend of knowledge, skills and technical (craft) ability with passion, commitment and 'stickability'. An important factor that links organisational leadership with the work of the creative artist is the moral imperative. There are numerous examples of art, literature and music that have been inspired by deeply held ethics or principles. It might be that creativity in school leadership is driven by the moral imperative to secure equity, to create an education system that is committed to social justice, to abandon the 19th century paradigm of schooling and replace it with a model based on 21st century learning.

Sadly, some leadership training still approaches the topic as if it were a simple list of qualities that need to be ticked off. Leadership is not a simple ladder to be climbed. Leadership is a complex mix of challenges and restrictions which require creativity to solve.

Key questions

Do you share Sternberg's and Perkins's views of the nature of leadership for creativity?

In appointing senior staff, how do you look for evidence of creativity?

How does the senior team build creative and innovative thinking into its day-to-day working?

Do you practice creativity in other aspects of your life (e.g. creative and performing arts and crafts)?

How do you encourage and support creativity for your staff and pupils?

Do you encourage creative artists and workers to come into school?

Have you ever devoted continuing professional development (CPD) sessions to exploring the dynamics of creativity?

Resources (CD-ROM)

C1(i)	The snowflake model of creativity
C1(ii)	A creativity plan for your school

2 Creating a research and inquiry based culture

Question

Can you find the answers from within your own organisation?

Why is this important?

If, through carrying out our own research, we can build our own knowledge and find more bespoke solutions, the process must be a clear win-win.

Key quotes for the section

> We believe it is time for educators – both academics and practitioners – to stop apologising for our research and clinging to paradigms that do not fit our reality.
>
> **(Anderson et al., 2007: xix)**

> What is needed is a profession that constantly and collectively builds its knowledge base and corresponding expertise, where practices and their impact are transparently tested, developed, circulated and adapted. There needs to be a continuous amalgamation of precision and innovation, as well as inquiry, improvisation and experimentation.
>
> **(Hargreaves and Fullan, 2012: 50)**

Section discussion (CD-ROM)

The stereotyped description of a university as dreaming spires, a remote and hallowed turf where knowledge is cultivated, has led to an acceptance for many that research is something done by others. You are told what to do as a result of research rather than being actively involved in it yourself. Thankfully, recent generations have started to realise that by involving school staff (and even pupils) in the process, a wealth of 'new' information can be created; information which is context and community specific and capable of supporting system change.

This area has even spawned its own language, and there are now many studies on practitioner research, action research, teacher inquiry and even participatory action research. Whatever we choose to call it, the first step is to recognise the huge potential that it holds for your organisation, and to make a commitment to develop a culture which will support and nurture this type of approach. If you allow your team to stumble into the swamp of literature on the topic, it would be easy for them to be put off before they begin, deterred by lists of dos and don'ts that can serve to create a myth around the subject. While there is no question that an understanding of the ethical issues surrounding research in the classroom is essential, some writers are guilty of making it overly complex, perhaps in a desire to add gravitas to their own work.

We will try to keep it simple by outlining a few straightforward steps by which you can develop a culture to support a positive approach:

1   Be clear why you wish to adopt a research/inquiry based approach.

2   Spread understanding of this approach across the school.

3   Share techniques that have been effective elsewhere.

4   Start small.

5   Discuss the findings across the whole school and refine the techniques used.

6   Develop systems for sharing the work over a sustained period.

7   Encourage engagement across the whole school.

8   Value the findings and coordinate your action.

The research techniques used to gather information are outlined in many publications (e.g. Menter et al., 2011). The most commonly used techniques include interviews, questionnaires, focus groups, observation, data analysis, photographic or video capture and diaries. Developing pockets of expertise within your school for each of the methods is effective for staff engagement, but it also ensures that your findings are obtained from a wide variety of research techniques.

Start by choosing a small team of enthusiasts who will demonstrate the potential of an inquiry approach by investigating issues relevant to most teachers. For example, 'How is the behaviour of my Year 9 boys effected by writing in files rather than notebooks?' or 'How is the learning of the times tables by pupils in Year 4 effected by holding the lesson outside?' Resource C2(i) is an effective tool to support this initial work. Once staff have decided on a question they should begin the planning, but quickly involve a research partner from within the school to help the teacher to approach the task thoroughly.

Once the research has been completed, encourage the teams to share their findings (even small ones) (resource C2(ii) will help with this) across the whole staff. Identify positives from any work carried out and encourage wider involvement in its findings. Produce an annual summary of your school's research – perhaps hold a conference to celebrate your work. Everything should be done to encourage staff to make this approach a natural part of their work.

Key questions

> Do you want to create a culture supportive to research/inquiry? Why?

> Which areas of your school could benefit from this approach?

> Which members of staff would be the most receptive in the initial stages?

Resources (CD-ROM)

C2(i)	Inquiry planning
C2(ii)	Inquiry findings

3   Organisational change and personal change

Question

What personal qualities does the leadership of change require?

Why is this important?

It is not enough to manage change as an event. The leadership of change requires personal and moral commitment and, pivotally, emotional engagement with the change process. It is impossible to lead a process of transformation without an equivalent level of personal change. This is the movement away from change as something done to others towards change as a collective experience. Authentic leadership that is rooted in trust and credibility must be internally consistent and demonstrate that the most significant change is personal and not just structural or organisational.

Key quote for the section

> I discern two legitimate reasons for undertaking new educational practices. The first reason is that current practices are not actually working ...
> The second reason is that conditions in the world are changing significantly. Consequent on these changes, certain goals, capacities, and practices might no longer be indicated, or even come to be seen as counterproductive.
>
> **(Gardner, 2006: 10)**

Section discussion (CD-ROM)

One of the key precepts of moral leadership is the axiom, 'Do as I do, not as I say.' Equally significant is the abundant evidence that change that is imposed from above rarely works. At best it secures grudging compliance; at worst outright rejection and the collapse of trust and commitment. As Gandhi famously said, 'You must be the change you wish to see in the world.'

The leadership of change would therefore seem to require leadership that is rooted in authenticity and integrity. It is only when people trust and believe in leaders that they are likely to make the commitment that is the essence of sustainable and deeply embedded change. This is particularly true when the change process involves complex and highly significant professional matters, such as classroom practice, that are often deeply rooted in personal experience, self-belief and confidence. In essence, every change process potentially involves the loss of personal history or the denial of historical practice. Asking me to change my practice actually involves asking me to change who I am. The more extensive my personal history, the less likely I am to risk compromising it. Successful change often involves the realignment of intrinsic motivation (e.g. stopping smoking, losing weight).

The change process is a highly subjective experience – there is no rationality or objectivity. *Managing* change often involves the rationalistic fallacy that change is a logical process that can be planned, controlled and predicted. If we reflect on our own lives, very few of us can say, at the age of say 40, that we are at a place, in terms of our personal and professional life, that we planned for at the age of 21. Many of our life choices are determined by random accidents, coincidences and choices that only make sense with the benefit of hindsight.

If this perspective on leading change is broadly accepted then it would seem appropriate to suggest that the leadership of change requires the following qualities, in varying quantities according to context and the nature of the change:

→ The ability to tolerate ambiguity and work with competing rationalities, multiple perceptions of reality and subjectivity.

→ A deep understanding of the nature of motivation and recognition of the range of alternative motivations in any group.

→ The skills and behaviours associated with negotiation, building consensus and securing alignment around core beliefs.

→ Absolute transparency and openness in the development of strategies to lead change and innovation.

→ Recognition and respect of alternative perspectives.

Resource C3(i) offers you an opportunity to consider you own approach to change. For each statement identify your own position on the line. The further your crosses are to the right, the greater your propensity for change. Produce a composite result for the whole leadership team. It is healthy to have a range of views within the group – in fact, there is real strength in having members in the team who have different views. By comparing different attitudes, the team (and the discussions) become stronger.

C3

Key questions

What is your experience of personal change? What is your emotional response to change in your life? Do you embrace or avoid change?

What are the characteristics of the most successful changes in education with which you have been involved?

What has been your most negative experience of change in any professional context?

Are schools different to other organisations in terms of the leadership of change?

Resources (CD-ROM)

C3(i)   Investigating attitudes to change

4   Encouraging risk taking

Question

How can we develop a risk taking culture in our schools?

Why is this important?

Without risk we have acceptance of the norm. With risk there is danger of failure. Understanding the benefits of calculated risk is an important tool in the armoury of any leadership team.

Key quotes for the section

> Do not be too timid and squeamish about your actions. All life is an experiment. The more experiments you make the better.
>
> **(Ralph Waldo Emerson)**

> A ship is always safe at the shore – but that is not what it is built for.
>
> **(Albert Einstein)**

> If you're not prepared to be wrong, it's unlikely that you'll ever come up with anything original.
>
> **(Robinson, 2001: 153)**

Section discussion (CD-ROM)

A cursory browse through the education pages of our national newspapers might lead us to believe that we live in a society that doesn't approve of risk taking. Failure to jump through the latest hoops is seen as the ultimate measure of failure, and schools 'doing things like they have always been done' continue to be the most celebrated. However, demonstrating a severe case of national policy ambiguity, the government expresses that in actual fact it *does* want its teaching leaders to be innovative and brave. The National Professional Qualification for Headship (NPQH) identifies risk taking as an important skill for leaders, and case studies of long term educational improvement all have elements of risk at their core. Some of our politicians claim that they want schools to be 'imaginative' and even Ofsted has taken to downgrading teachers for 'playing it safe'.

So, if the leadership team are serious about trying to generate long term improvement, they must create a climate in which risk taking will occur. A climate where new ideas are welcomed and the 'safe' choice is not the only default. A climate where teachers open their doors to new ideas (and people) and not one where pupils copy learning objectives into their exercise books in silence.

The starting point for your journey into the wild side of education must be to decide how much risk taking already occurs in your school. Sadly, you may not be the best person to judge this – leaders often seriously overestimate the amount of risk taking that happens on a daily basis. Many believe they are daredevils at the cutting edge of education, when in fact they are wearing a safety harness and are well away from danger. Why not find out from those most involved in any risk, the staff and pupils? A possible set of questions is included in resource C4(i) (for staff) and C4(ii) (for pupils). To encourage honesty in their responses, ensure that anonymity is guaranteed for all those completing the questionnaire. Discuss the findings at a team meeting.

If the conclusion of your survey is that the school should develop a less risk averse culture, then the first step might be to begin a conversation at a staff meeting about the nature of risk, and why some risk is a good thing. Issue the first page of C4(iii) along with pairs of scissors. Ask staff to cut up the table and order the 16 eventualities from the highest risk down to the lowest risk. Once completed, issue the answer sheet (the second page), which contains the calculated risk and ranking order. Encourage a discussion about how good a judge of risk we are. Which eventuality on the list does it seem most sensible to take action in order to prevent? For example, it would be far more logical for an individual to adopt measures that might reduce cancer than to spend money on protecting themselves from mountain lions!

Ask staff to generate a list of things that they would like to see the school do, and write them on sticky notes. Then ask them to place the notes on a 'continuum of risk' from most to least desirable. Record the produced list and circulate it to staff. At the next leadership team meeting, ask each member of the team to identify three risks they think are worth exploring further. Discuss the relative merits and develop a 'top five risks worth taking' for the school. Producing the list in itself will start to develop a recognition that playing things safe is perhaps not the best way forward for the school. However, a productive risk taking culture cannot develop without a considerable level of trust and empathy being demonstrated by leaders on a daily basis. Staff need to be given permission, not just in words, but in practical ways that are demonstrated daily. Praise must be focused on staff who try new things, whether successful or not. Why not produce a weekly risk bulletin, a bravery board, 'I've been brave' badges or appoint a head of risk?

Key questions

How risk averse is your school?

Do you believe that taking more risks would help your school to develop?

Do the staff feel they can take risks in the way they teach?

Are there examples in the school of risks that have produced benefit? Do you celebrate them?

Resources (CD-ROM)

C4(i)	How risk averse is your school? (Staff)
C4(ii)	How risk averse is your school? (Pupil)
C4(iii)	Staff activity cards

5   Structure vs. freedom

Question

How do school leaders achieve an appropriate balance between control and trust, structure and freedom, tight and loose?

Why is this important?

Working with young people, especially teenagers, is a delicate balancing act of control and trust. At times there need to be very explicit boundaries with clearly defined requirements. At other times there are situations where there is trust and loosely defined expectations. Teams and schools are no different. There are certain non-negotiables that have to be guaranteed if the school is to work (e.g. the infrastructure has to be secure) but, equally, there have to be opportunities for creativity, experimentation and innovation.

Key quotes for the section

> [Innovative communities] seem to combine many ingredients that are traditionally kept separate, or at least prove difficult to combine. There is healthy competition within the community but also cooperation and sharing; it thrives on masses of individual initiative but is founded on a public good, ... the community is highly distributed and virtual, yet also hierarchical, with a single authority at its heart.
>
> **(Leadbeater, 2003: 41)**

> It is no longer possible to rely on linear models of management. Linear models of management, which underpinned the simple linear causality of the command and control mentality of hierarchical, bureaucratic organizations, have to be replaced with networked, nonlinear, emergent, mutually informing groups.
>
> **(Morrison, 2002: 16)**

Section discussion (CD-ROM)

The following section seeks to represent the tensions inherent in any team, organisation or community – the need to balance the freedom to innovate and be creative with the need for consistency and, central to any school improvement strategy, the need to secure consistency and eliminate variation.

The following is included as resource C5(i). On the diagram, indicate the proportion of time that you spend on tasks associated with every section of the graph. Compare

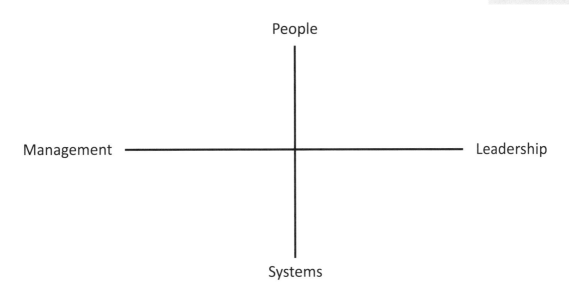

this with the rest of your team. What issues does this raise for the use of leadership time in your school?

Any great painting is a balance of the very formal techniques of drawing, perspective, colour theory and so on, which serve as the foundation for the artist's inspiration and originality, and the creativity that makes a work of art unique. Highly effective leadership is confident and comfortable in moving from bottom-left to top-right, but always on the basis that the basics are in place. One way of seeing this, as the classic maxim says, is that leadership is about doing the right things and management about doing things right. Management and leadership are in a symbiotic relationship – both are essential. It is the ratio between them that makes all the difference to school improvement.

Use resource C5(ii) to examine your own leadership further and to consider where you find equilibrium in the daily tensions between tight vs. loose, improvement vs. transformation, control vs. trust and conformity vs. creativity. Once you have thought about where you are currently operating, use the form to identify any changes you wish to make to that balance. In the first instance, this should be personal, and then it should be based around the needs of the whole team. Does everyone have to see balance in the same way? If they don't, hiding this difference is certainly not the way forward.

Another way of conceptualising the relationship between structure and freedom is to think in terms of mature and immature organisations. True creativity and innovation

57

C5

require high trust and a culture that encourages risk taking. Use resource C5(iii) to gather evidence about the current maturity of your school and any issues that you can identify to improve this. Talk to your staff about the ways that you can all 'mature'. Help the wider school understand that any organisation is on a journey, and that understanding where they are helps to remove many stresses – and hopefully avoids being asked the question, 'Are we there yet?', at every turn!

Key questions

How can you encourage 'heresy'?

Who are the school's most innovative teachers, and how do you recognise and reinforce their creativity?

What status and significance is attached to pupils' ideas and insights about their learning?

How does your professional development policy support and encourage innovation in teaching and learning?

How many of your colleagues are comfortable with researching and introducing new pedagogies?

Are the creative arts given the same status as the curriculum basics?

Which aspects of the school's life celebrate creativity?

Resources (CD-ROM)

C5(i)	Demands placed on leaders
C5(ii)	Finding the leadership balance
C5(iii)	Organisational maturity

Leading teaching and learning

1   Equity, fairness, vulnerable students and closing the gap

Question

What can leaders do to create a fair school which all pupils have the potential to benefit from?

Why is this important?

Imagine schooling that isn't fair – schooling that only favours the advantaged, schooling that deliberately discriminates. Few of us would feel comfortable working in such a school, even though some would claim that many schools are walking blindly into this very scenario.

The optimal situation for a school, or an education system, is to achieve both equity and excellence. But there are some who believe that these factors are mutually exclusive. One problem with some education systems is that they are democratic (i.e. every young person has the right to go to school) but they lack equity (i.e. not every young person goes to a good school).

Key quotes for the section

> My mother said I must always be intolerant of ignorance but understanding of illiteracy. That some people, unable to go to school, were more educated and more intelligent than college professors.
>
> **(Attributed to Maya Angelou)**

Section discussion (CD-ROM)

Any teacher, if asked, 'Is every child you teach identical?', would undoubtedly quickly tell you that it was a stupid question and that, of course, they were not. However, lesson observations might sometimes lead us to ask the question again. Teaching a lesson from the front, with a single point of entry and assuming a step-by-step approach appears to presuppose the training of a group of automatons.

D1

Politicians around the world have raised concerns about the poor performance of pupils from deprived/minority families. The fact that research analysing the factors which influence pupil learning has identified that 80% stem from social and personal factors outside the school should not deter us. Particularly in conjunction with the fact that the variation *within* most schools is still greater than the variation *between* social factors. In other words, improving the performance within your school remains crucial. Researchers have identified five priorities for schools that wish to close the gap.

1 Share the values

What are you doing, and why? Ensure ethos is not simply a catchy phrase that is trotted out for prospective parents, but is like the writing in a stick of rock – running through everything you do. How explicit is your commitment to securing fairness and equity? Do you discriminate in favour of the most vulnerable children? To what extent is the quality of teaching and learning consistent across the whole school? How confident are you that your school's values are embedded in the daily life of every member of the school community? (See section A2 if you feel your ethos still needs work!)

2 Develop trust

In their research into elementary schools in Chicago, Bryk and Schneider (2002) found a high correlation between the levels of trust in a school and its capacity to improve. Schools with a high level of trust had a one in two chance of improving in maths and literacy, while schools with low levels of trust had only a one in seven chance. How could you develop trust within your school? Do you have a handle on the levels of trust at each level of your organisation? Use D1(i) to investigate.

3 Develop quality professional learning

Brandell Robinson (2011) identified the factors that affect the quality of professional learning (see D1(ii)). It is a stark lesson for leaders. By a considerable margin, the biggest influence a leader can have is to promote the learning and to join in the learning themselves. So, the next time you excuse yourself from some training to do something more important – *don't*! (See also D1(iii) and section F4.)

4 Learning centred leadership

Southworth (2004) defined three elements of learning centred leadership.

1 *Modelling:* Do as you say you expect others to do.

2 *Monitoring:* Analysing what everyone does and what needs to be done.

3 *Dialogue:* Creating opportunities for professional dialogues at all levels.

The goal is to find the overlap between these three elements – what we refer to as coaching and mentoring. Use D1(iv) to analyse your own behaviours, and consider what you can do to be a more effective coach or mentor.

5 Move from find and fix to predict and prevent

Predict and prevent is essentially the same as prevention is better than cure. It involves moving the culture of a team or department from reaction to anticipation and intervention – crucially, the willingness to intervene. There are numerous instances of this approach in everyday life. For example, the best way to avoid a heart attack is to stop smoking, not to invest in more cardiac surgeons. And the most effective way to maintain your car's efficiency is to have it regularly serviced.

Do you service your school? Use resource D1(v) to find out.

Key questions

Is everyone in your school treated with equal respect?

How consistent is the ethos in the school (ask pupils, staff, governors and parents)?

Is there a climate of trust in your school?

Is your training continuing professional development (CPD) or joint practice development (JPD)?

How do you classify your leadership?

Are you predicting or reacting?

Resources (CD-ROM)

D1(i)	Levels of trust	D1(iv)	Coaching and mentoring
D1(ii)	Factors influencing high quality teaching and learning	D1(v)	Leadership strategies to close the gap
D1(iii)	CPD vs. JPD		

D2

2   Leading dialogue about teaching and learning

Question

How do leaders build a common understanding and shared vocabulary around teaching and learning?

Why is this important?

Leaders are often at their most effective when they are actively engaged in dialogue with their colleagues. Dialogue is important in two respects. First, it is a vital means of building effective personal relationships, trust and consensus. Second, it enables leaders to obtain feedback and work towards building shared understanding and confidence. A commitment to ensuring that learning conversations are taking place with all members of the school community is a very powerful way to create a learning culture.

Key quotes for the section

> Conversation is a meeting of minds with different memories and habits. When minds meet, they don't just exchange facts: they transform them, reshape them, draw different implications from them, and engage in new trains of thought. Conversation doesn't just reshuffle the cards: it creates new cards … It's like a spark that two minds create.
>
> **(Zeldin, 1998: 14)**

> Dialogue … is an art and a discipline that deepens and grows more meaningful the more we engage in it. Dialogue also gets better the more we try out different moves and experiment with a variety of ways to listen more fully, speak more fluently from the heart, communicate more coherently, affirm more generously and learn more lastingly from those around us.
>
> **(West-Burnham et al., 2007: 89)**

Section discussion (CD-ROM)

'We need to talk' are four words that can be the commencement to some very diverse outcomes – from heartbreak to enlightenment and understanding. Good dialogue is characterised by genuine reciprocity. It is a two-way process in which there is a shared and equal commitment to respect the dignity and integrity of each of the participants. Dialogues are essentially egalitarian; they have to be characterised by parity of esteem. The purpose of the dialogue is to achieve a mutual understanding via the testing of alternative hypotheses, the exclusion of inappropriate arguments and fallacious conclusions and the generation of creative strategies. A dialogue is about the achievement of shared understanding, not the winning of a debate, which implies winners and losers. While there are many types of dialogue, ranging from the personal and intimate to community wide conversations, in the context of leading teaching and learning two approaches are particularly significant: professional and learning dialogues.

Professional dialogue

Professional dialogue is the discourse of work and the sharing of expertise; the discussion between doctor and doctor, the master instructing the apprentice, the academics debating, the engineers problem solving. In one sense, dialogue in this context is characterised by a closed 'expert' language, a specialist vocabulary – jargon to the outsider.

Use chart D2(i) to collect the jargon used within your school. Discussion is greatly limited if contributors are using different vocabulary. Identify areas where ambiguity is possible and make a concerted effort to adopt certain phrases consistently across the school.

Dialogue is about public communication too – the writer, the journalist and the professional communicator. This is also the language of leadership – the dialogue about values, the discourse on purpose, the questioning of technique and professional practice. Leaders are often at their most effective when they are actively seeking opportunities to engage in dialogue; sometimes briefly and informally, sometimes in great detail in a formal setting.

The first step is to analyse your actual practice. Many of us have the best intentions but will often find 'more important' ways to fill our time. Complete D2(ii) as an individual exercise and then collate your findings across the leadership team. Are you happy with the picture it paints? Are your dialogues too focused on behaviour? Are they generally only among leaders? Decide what dialogues you want to be having and chart your progress towards this.

Learning dialogue

A learning dialogue is manifested in the process of mentoring, coaching and tutoring. It is also the language of facilitation and teaching. It is characterised by inquiry, discovery, questioning, challenge and support, nurturing, explaining and affirming. This is when the leader assumes the role of coach or mentor and works with a colleague to enhance their performance or understanding. This is a conversation with purpose – a purpose that should be evident to both mentor and mentee. Use resource D2(iii) to consider the learning dialogues that occur in your school. Are they planned? Are they all carried out in a similar way? Do they have agreed guidelines? Are they effective? Make answering these questions a priority. As a leadership team, this is an area where you can make quick improvements.

Effective dialogues can be very informal (e.g. a quick word in passing on the corridor), very structured and formal (e.g. a coaching session) and can involve all members of the school community. While leadership led dialogues are very important, leaders should not have a monopoly on this strategy. Dialogues between staff and between staff and pupils are potentially very powerful.

Key questions

To what extent are you personally comfortable engaging in genuine dialogue with colleagues about teaching and learning?

To what extent does your leadership team model effective dialogue in its own working routines and procedures?

Does the school have a shared vocabulary for talking about teaching and learning?

Are pupils involved in dialogue about their own learning and their experience as learners in the school?

How much time, over a given period, have school leaders devoted to dialogue with colleagues? Has every member of staff been involved in some sort of professional conversation on a regular basis?

How do you encourage learning conversations across the staff, especially across age ranges and subject teaching teams?

Resources (CD-ROM)

D2(i)	Collecting the jargon
D2(ii)	Charting dialogues
D2(iii)	Recording learning dialogues

D3

3   Securing learner engagement

Question

Are your systems supporting and nurturing learner engagement or actually hampering it?

Why is this important?

Engaged pupils are better behaved and more likely to be self-motivated. They enable teachers to create a more imaginative learning environment and to improve the experience for all. A motivated pupil is more likely to spark interest in other pupils than the class teacher.

Key quotes for the section

> The more engaged students are the less they will experience burnout and in turn less likely to drop out. The demands that are placed on the students in the classroom should allow for a variety of learning opportunities. The more resources that students have the less likely they will burn out and the more likely they will be engaged.
>
> **(Alarcon et al., 2011: 211)**

> Student engagement is the product of motivation and active learning. It is a product rather than a sum because it will not occur if either element is missing.
>
> **(Barkley, 2010: 6)**

Section discussion (CD-ROM)

If you walk around your school and look into the classrooms, do you see engagement? Is there an exciting buzz as learners and teacher interact around a topic, or does it feel more akin to a battle, where learning was the first victim? Probably the reality is somewhere in between; some engagement and some battle hardened warriors. You are also likely to see different levels of involvement from pupils, which means a simple 'yes' or 'no' classification is unhelpful.

Schlechty (2002: xiv) defines five levels of student engagement:

1   *Authentic engagement* – students are immersed in work that has clear meaning and immediate value to them (e.g. reading a book on a topic of personal interest).

2   *Ritual compliance* – the work has little or no immediate meaning to students, but there are extrinsic outcomes of value that keep them engaged (e.g. earning grades necessary for college acceptance).

3   *Passive compliance* – students see little or no meaning in the assigned work but expend effort merely to avoid negative consequences (e.g. not having to stay in during break to complete work).

4   *Retreatism* – students are disengaged from assigned work and make no attempt to comply, but are not disruptive to the learning of others.

5   *Rebellion* – students refuse to do the assigned task, act disruptively and attempt to substitute alternative activities.

Use D3(i) to identify the percentage of engagement you observe in any class at a particular moment. Use this to help your staff to identify levels of engagement in their classes and then involve them in discussion about what is leading to any disengagement.

Factors effecting engagement

→ *Pupil choice – do they have to be there?*

It is a natural human trait: we don't like to be told something is good for us and to feel as if we have little or no control over the issue. So why should pupils be any different? This creates an issue for many of us. Most pupils sit before you not because it is something they desire but because they have been told they must.

So what can we do? You may not be able to eliminate the compulsory nature of your lessons but introduce as much negotiation as possible (e.g. what order you learn the topics in, what method of learning you use for each topic, ways of splitting the lesson into sections).

→ *Personal characteristics*

How well-organised and self-motivated are the pupils already? Teachers sometimes believe that this is just what you have to put up with (the 'kids around here' syndrome), rather than realising that this is an area where teacher skill comes to the fore.

So what can we do? Personalisation may be an overused term, but this is exactly the area where it is most needed. Rewriting a task to make it more directly relevant to students can produce dramatic changes in levels of engagement, as can encouraging students to prepare their own resources. Research has found that handwritten tasks are more engaging for some pupils.

D3

→ *Class dynamics*

Does the make-up of individuals in the class contribute to or detract from engagement? Are pupils reluctant to give wrong (or right) answers in front of their classmates?

So what can we do? Some leadership teams are experimenting with single sex groupings to try to lessen this problem, but it can also be improved within the room by rearranging internal groupings and seating. Seating plans can be used positively to promote engagement rather than simply to control behaviour. Encourage discussion, breaking into small groups for directed discussion and voting. Also consider developing online work – discussion boards, correctly managed, can help pupils to engage away from the classroom.

→ *Relevance of material*

Is this work of immediate relevance to the pupil? We all know that some lesson topics are of more interest to young people than others. Too many teachers allow this to affect them and approach the lesson in a resigned manner. 'We have to cover this – it's on the syllabus and they always ask questions on it,' is a green light for student disinterest.

So what can we do? Introducing humour into the topic is a natural route. Rather than being the first step on a slippery slope to misbehaviour, smiling and laughter are just as likely to herald an interest in learning. The chemicals produced in the process stimulate curiosity and involvement. Also develop feedback mechanisms, such as the use of coloured cards, thumbs up/down or even electronic pads, to encourage pupil response and to let you know how things are going.

→ *Teacher engagement*

If the teacher isn't interested, how on earth can we expect the pupils to make the learning leap? It may be hard to believe, but we have heard experienced teachers tell a class that the topic was boring, as if knowing this would somehow help! This is akin to a restaurant advertising its food as tasteless and potentially dangerous.

So what can we do? Simple – if a topic really is essential, teachers *must* find an angle to make it interesting for themselves. Try introducing some pace: slow delivery is a feedback loop which may emphasise your disinterest. Include more physical activities (e.g. 'Move to this side/corner if you think this answer is correct'). Use games and media to deliver the concepts and, even better, to stimulate a meaningful plenary session.

Develop your engagement strategies using resource D3(ii).

Key questions

To what extent are your pupils fully engaged?

Do you analyse different depths of pupil engagement in the classroom?

Are staff focused on raising engagement levels in their classes?

Do staff share strategies for improving pupil engagement?

Do you ever investigate staff engagement?

Resources (CD-ROM)

D3(i)	Engagement observation log
D3(ii)	Improving pupil engagement

4   Models of learning

Question

Are you confident that every pupil is learning to optimal effect all of the time?

Why is this important?

Most education systems have high confidence about what is to be taught and how it should be taught. There is less confidence as to whether pupils are actually learning. For many years, the focus has been on the teacher teaching rather than the learner learning. Some schools are changing in this respect (for example, secondary schools have moved from deputy head of curriculum to deputy head of learning) but there is still a vacuum in many schools in terms of agreed principles around the nature of learning.

Key quotes for the section

> How do we think children can be best placed to learn? Do we want to see them learning as a transmission process, where, in the main, teachers transmit and pupils receive and they either get it or they are bored or they don't understand or they couldn't care less? Would we rather learning were an experience like a greasy pole, where eventually youngsters are expected to be unable to hold on any longer? Or do we want it to be a sticky experience where children are sucked into learning and unable to let go? What sort of teachers will be needed to make learning authentic and enable it to come alive?
>
> (Waters, 2013: 307–308)

Section discussion (CD-ROM)

Most assessment in education is summative and this leads to a model of learning that is essentially instrumental and reductionist – teaching to pass the test. An alternative approach is to teach in order to secure confidence about the basic information, but then to enhance the learning of the individual so that they understand what has been taught. The movement from the shallow learning of 'knowing what' to the deep learning of 'knowing why'.

In order to achieve deep learning for all, there needs to be a consensus between learners, their parents and their teachers around the fundamental assumptions underpinning successful learning. Such a consensus might include the following elements:

→ *Every learner is unique*. Each learner has a distinctive history and a personal profile that informs their engagement with every aspect of school. Their inheritance is the result of a complex interaction of nature and nurture. Understanding the distinctive profile of every individual is an essential precursor to effective engagement which, in turn, implies learner choice and control, personal pathways and focused interventions that reinforce the intrinsic motivation and ambition of each learner.

→ *Learning is a social process*. The quality of personal relationships between learners and teachers, and learners and learners is an essential prerequisite to successful learning. Learners need different permutations of social situations/skills to maximise learning opportunities, especially collaborative projects and high quality interaction.

→ *Intelligence can be learned*. The scientific evidence is compelling: intelligence is not fixed. The use of cognitive strategies, such as learning to think, metacognitive approaches and problem solving based learning, can have a positive impact on a pupil's potential.

→ *Learning is a neurological function*. Learning is the result of changes in the brain, and there are aspects of effective learning that can be used to enhance neurological engagement. For example, memory is a fundamental component of summative assessment and memory can be developed. Equally, challenge is an essential element of motivation and engagement and can help to develop focus and concentration.

→ *Learning can take place anytime, anywhere, with anyone*. Pupils spend about 15% of each year in school. This means that the vast majority of learning takes place outside school, notably in the family, the community and with peers – children are never not learning! This raises the issue of parents as co-educators and recognising the community as a learning resource.

→ *Learning is assessed through understanding*. Assessment has to be a formative process based on effective feedback that builds confidence and understanding and, critically, enables the learner to actually apply their learning – to speak the language, to use maths in real situations and to grow in confidence. This means assessment for learning that is an essentially formative and negotiated process that is driven by the learner.

→ *Teaching enables learning*. The crucial criterion for effective teaching is that every pupil understands and makes progress so that achievement improves for all. This involves the teacher designing learning strategies in response to the needs of pupils,

D4

not the demands of the topic or their personal preferred teaching style. This might entail the teacher working as mentor/coach or moving into a facilitative role. This, in turn, implies that the teacher has a wide repertoire of strategies that can be deployed in response to the needs of learners.

Ask your pupils to complete a questionnaire to find out their views of the learning experience at your school, using the areas identified (D4(i) is a template which you may wish to amend for your own circumstances). Hand out a similar resource (D4(ii)) to a selection of staff and ask them to predict the replies you will receive from the majority of pupils. Look at these results during a leadership team meeting and then jointly complete the score sheet (D4(iii)), which will help you to develop your priorities for the coming year.

Key questions

What evidence is there that the school's strategies start with the needs of the individual, especially the most vulnerable and disadvantaged?

How confident are you about the quality of interpersonal relationships across the school?

Are techniques to develop cognitive capacity used consistently across the whole school?

Are challenge and problem solving dominant features of the pupil experience?

Is learning seen as a collaborative process involving families and the wider community?

Is assessment for learning used appropriately by all staff?

Does teaching enable deep learning for all pupils?

Resources (CD-ROM)

D4(i)	Teaching and learning strategies (pupils)
D4(ii)	Teaching and learning strategies (staff assessments of pupils' views)
D4(iii)	Teaching and learning strategies (leaders)

5   Models of teaching

Question

With so many possible models of teaching, is your approach to teaching and learning fit for purpose?

Why is this important?

The quality of teaching and learning in a school is a fundamental driver to its success. Are you stumbling into a particular model of teaching, or are your teaching strategies finely tuned to the needs of your pupils?

Key quotes for the section

> The models are guides to the preparation and implementation of teaching, and not highly developed theories.
>
> **(Brady, 1985: 1)**

> I suppose it is tempting, if the only tool you have is a hammer, to treat everything as if it were a nail.
>
> **(Maslow, 1966: 15)**

Section discussion (CD-ROM)

Whether you are in a school which puts all its faith in a particular teaching model or a school which follows the latest fad, this section should be of benefit to you. Knowledge of a variety of models will lead you to greater teaching flexibility and efficiency. Understanding several models could facilitate the ability to adapt those models or to combine them with others, thereby utilising valuable approaches that will enrich any teacher's repertoire.

To develop Maslow's hammer and nail analogy, the more tools in your toolbox, the greater the opportunity you will have to choose the most appropriate tool for the task at hand. Highly successful teachers have a wide repertoire of strategies to call on to ensure that every pupil is actively engaged in appropriate tasks and that the mode of learning is directly relevant to the topic being studied. As with all crafts, it is the willingness to use a wide range of tools and techniques that is the foundation of real expertise.

A very brief summary of some of the most popular models are:

→ *Direct instruction*. Direct instruction is a highly structured model which is used most effectively when teaching basic skills, such as reading and mathematics, when the tasks to be learned can be broken into small discrete chunks.

→ *Concept attainment*. By teaching the thinking skill of categorising, students comprehend and analyse the meaning of particular concepts. Through a series of positive and negative examples, students define the concept and determine its essential attributes.

→ *Concept development*. The concept development model teaches students to group data based on perceived similarities and then to form categories and labels for that data, effectively producing a conceptual system.

→ *Synectics*. Synectics uses group interaction to stimulate creative thought through metaphorical analogies. Far from being a lonely, isolated process, creative thinking and expression become group activities in which each individual can participate.

→ *Suchman Inquiry*. In this model, learners take a puzzling situation and follow a scientific process that leads to a hypothesis. Learners are encouraged to seek more than one answer to a question.

→ *Classroom discussion*. The discussion model guides the planning and selection of questions to be used in classroom discussions. Both students and teachers learn to identify different levels and types of questions.

→ *Vocabulary acquisition*. This model presents the exciting possibility of teaching vocabulary through the history of language and word derivation rather than by memorising lists.

→ *Cooperative learning*. Cooperative learning models (e.g. Teams–Games–Tournament (TGT), Student Teams–Academic Divisions (STAD), Jigsaw, Think–Pair–Share) describe ways in which the teacher can encourage students to work with and help other students in the classroom.

→ *Memory models*. Memory models (which include a link, loci, memory through motion, names and faces) provide techniques through which both teachers and students can improve their memory skills. Good memory can be developed and all learners should have access to this process.

→ *Conflict resolution*. Help students to understand their own feelings as they learn to explore the feelings of others in real-life situations as well as in literature.

D5

Of all these potential methods, which, if any, would be of use to you? The key is to explore the effect of your current strategy. Use resource D5(i) to compile evidence from lesson observations, achievement, performance management and the school development plan. Enter your observations in the Venn diagram, comparing what pupils need, what staff feel they deliver and what is actually happening on a day-to-day basis. Is there cohesiveness to your work, or is it the educational equivalent of a paint-ball attack (an excess in some aspects and nothing in others)? Once you have decided if your current approach is delivering what you need, you can consider if a new teaching model is needed. Use D5(ii) to match your identified needs to the next steps for your strategy.

Key questions

What models of teaching do you have in your school? Why is this?

Are these models effective? If not, why are they still being used?

What new teaching strategies are you going to focus on?

Resources (CD-ROM)

| D5(i) | Is teaching and learning working? |
| D5(ii) | Making use of models of teaching |

6   Improving teaching and learning

Question

Which leadership strategies are likely to have the greatest impact on the quality of teaching and learning?

Why is this important?

It is probably the case that the quality of teaching and learning is the central and most significant aspect of school leadership – it is difficult to imagine the case for anything else as having the same significance. Morally, there can be little doubt that securing equity in terms of access to effective teaching and learning is the major imperative for school leaders. In terms of accountability, teaching and learning are the central issues for school leaders and governors.

Key quotes for the section

> [T]hen trust represents the social energy, or the 'oven's heat,' necessary for transforming these basic ingredients into comprehensive school change. Absent the social energy provided by trust, improvement initiatives are unlikely to culminate in meaningful change, regardless of their intrinsic merit.
>
> **(Bryk et al., 2010: 157)**

> The main conclusion to be drawn from the present analyses is that particular types of school leadership have substantial impacts on student outcomes. The more leaders focus their influence, their learning, and their relationships with teachers on the core business of teaching and learning, the greater their likely influence on student outcomes.
>
> **(Robinson, 2011: 27)**

Section discussion (CD-ROM)

So, if we all agree on the importance of the leader's role in focusing our colleagues on their practice, what strategies are most effective at doing this? The very detailed and authoritative research carried out by Bryk et al. and Robinson provides us with very clear guidelines as to the highest impact strategies in terms of securing consistently high quality teaching and learning. Robinson's work points to the dominant significance of leaders being active in the learning and development of their staff. For Bryk, it is the quality of relationships that acts as the pivotal catalyst for school improvement. In both cases, it is the level of interaction of leaders with their colleagues that seems to make the difference.

Analyse the minutes of your last five leadership team meetings. Roughly what percentage of your time was dedicated to aspects of teaching and learning? Does this indicate that you are giving enough importance to this aspect?

Bryk et al. centre their research on the quality of relationships, arguing that it is trust that serves as the catalyst for improvements in teaching and learning. The basic ingredients referred to in the previous quotation are the classic components of school improvement: effective leadership, engagement with parents, developing staff capacity, focusing on the student and putting teaching and learning at the centre of everything. However worthy these components are in and of themselves, or in combination, without trust, argues Bryk, they will not improve the quality of teaching and learning.

Use the resource D6(i) to analyse your own school improvement work and consider what evidence you can find of an ethos of trust. Try to identify ways that you can improve this further.

Southworth (2004) provides a more specific approach that is entirely consistent with Bryk et al. and Robinson. He argues that three leadership strategies have the highest potential to impact directly on the quality of teaching and learning: dialogue, modelling and monitoring. *Dialogue* might be best understood as learning conversations; leaders engaging with all members of the school community in talk about teaching and learning in order to help develop a common language and shared vocabulary, to ensure consistency, secure understanding and embed best practice. Leaders often underestimate how much significance colleagues attach to opportunities for dialogue with them. *Modelling* is one of the simplest leadership principles – 'do as I do' not 'do as I say'. People are more likely to change their practice on the basis of following rather than being directed. *Monitoring* involves leaders having high quality evidence on which to base judgements about the quality of teaching and learning. In essence, this involves engaging with the data that shows pupil attainment and progress, observing lessons and other learning activities and carrying out reviews of pupils' work.

There is a fourth element that is directly related to these three strategies: *coaching*. In many ways, dialogue, modelling and monitoring are central components of coaching, but it is worth stressing coaching itself as a distinctive leadership strategy that focuses on specific interventions to support and facilitate improvement in performance. This is a direct reflection of Robinson's point: leaders are highly effective in improving teaching and learning when they are actually employing effective learning strategies.

You probably read this list nodding sagely, hoping that you would effortlessly glide through all of these elements. A good starting point is to analyse your own leadership activities under these four headings (resource D6(ii) will help with this process). Once you have some data, compare this with the rest of your team. Is your leadership making the most of all four aspects?

Underpinning all of the above is a school culture that accentuates the centrality of learning, secures the entitlement of every learner to high quality learning experiences and expresses this culture through high aspirations and expectations for all. Hand out resource D6(iii) to your leadership team in advance of a meeting. Compile a composite of your team's effectiveness across these important aspects of school leadership and use this to focus the team's work for the coming term.

Key questions

> What evidence would you put forward to demonstrate the leadership team's commitment to learning?

> What conclusions might be drawn from the minutes of leadership team and governing body meetings about the centrality of teaching and learning in the school?

> Is this commitment reflected in the work of middle leaders?

> What examples do you have of the governing body holding the leadership team to account on matters relating to teaching and learning?

> How consistent is the understanding of teaching and learning across the school community?

> How active are pupils in securing high quality teaching and learning?

D6

Resources (CD-ROM)

D6(i)	Assessing school improvement work
D6(ii)	Personal leadership activities
D6(iii)	Leadership effectiveness

Leading and managing resources

1   Prevention is better than cure

Question

How should you maximise the effect of your resources? Which area of expenditure has greatest impact on the development of young people in your school?

Why is this important?

Schools have a finite budget which will never be enough. I doubt any head teacher anywhere in the world has ever returned a cheque to their government claiming that they couldn't find anything to spend it on! Every leadership team should be involved in budget setting and monitoring. This must not be a job only for the head teacher.

Key quotes for the section

> An ounce of prevention is better than a pound of cure.
>
> **(Attributed to Benjamin Franklin)**

> Economy does not lie in sparing money, but in spending it wisely.
>
> **(Thomas Henry Huxley)**

Section discussion (CD-ROM)

Andy Hargreaves tells an apocryphal story: imagine standing near a river where a succession of people keep bobbing past crying for help. Most schools have become very good at throwing in life jackets and dragging them to safety, but a few schools have the foresight to walk upstream and find out why so many are falling in!

This is exactly how an effective leadership team should be thinking: is spending money wisely early on cheaper and more effective than waiting to treat the problem later? The wisdom of this can be considered on two fronts, financial and human. Reflect on a problem you think might occur. Considered from a purely budgetary mindset, a simple set of questions need to be addressed. How much would it cost to fix it now? How likely is it that the problem is going to develop? How much will it cost to fix the problem when it manifests itself? How much money would you save over time if you managed to fix the problem now?

Of course, school leaders are not in the widget making profession, so financial benefit alone is not enough. The positive benefit that early expenditure would have on the pupils and the community may outweigh even a small financial loss, but where both human and financial arguments coalesce, this must be an issue for serious consideration.

The Sutton Trust-Education Endowment Foundation has produced a toolkit to help leadership teams to identify strategies to improve learning. A very useful part of this is a table of possible solutions linked to their potential impact and cost. The top seven in terms of relative cost benefit are:

	Approach	Potential gain	Overall Cost Benefit
1	Effective feedback	+9 months	Very high impact for low cost
2	Metacognition and self-regulation strategies	+8 months	High impact for low cost
3	Peer tutoring/peer assisted learning	+6 months	High impact for low cost
4	Early intervention	+6 months	High impact for very high cost
5	One-to-one tutoring	+5 months	Moderate impact for very high cost
6	Homework	+5 months	Moderate impact for very low cost
7	ICT	+4 months	Moderate impact for high cost

Rather controversially, one of the lowest scoring strategies was the use of teaching assistants which scored:

8	Teaching assistants	+1 month	Low impact for high cost

This work sets an interesting backdrop for any leadership team to begin considering their use of resources. While no research should be accepted without question, equally it should not be discarded in a similar fashion. Spending time considering a more complete version of the Sutton Trust-Education Endowment Foundation Toolkit would be valuable for any leadership team. Use E1(i) to gather your thoughts. Consider what areas of school development could most benefit from a 'prevention not cure' activity, then analyse what strategies may have a potential effect on this. Raising a forward thinking mentality across the whole school community can only improve whole school progress.

Key questions

Is your spending strategy based on reaction or prediction?

What issue, if solved, would be of maximum benefit to your pupils?

Would the expenditure be justified?

Are you currently spending money on a cure that is not effective?

Resources (CD-ROM)

E1(i)   Prevention strategies

For more on the Sutton Trust-Education Endowment Foundation Toolkit on teaching and learning visit: http://educationendowmentfoundation.org.uk/toolkit/.

2   Procedures and systems

Question

How do school leaders work to eliminate variation, ensure consistency and secure the entitlement of every pupil to effective learning?

Why is this important?

It is probably true to say that the biggest single barrier to equity in education, securing school improvement and creating outstanding schools is variation – the lack of consistency in terms of teaching and learning. Closely related to this issue is the associated problem of a teaching culture which focuses on finding and fixing rather than predicting and preventing. We all know that prevention is better than cure, yet many organisations wait until something goes wrong, and then try to put it right, rather than establishing systems that will help prevent failure.

Key quotes for the section

> Substantial parts of what software designers, financial managers, fire fighters, police officers, lawyers and most certainly clinicians do are now too complex for them to carry out reliably from memory alone. Multiple fields, in other words, have become too much airplane for one person to fly.
>
> Yet is far from obvious that something as simple as a checklist could be of substantial help. We may admit that errors and oversights occur – even devastating ones. But we believe our jobs are too complicated to reduce to a checklist. Sick people, for instance, are phenomenally more various than airplanes. A study of forty one thousand trauma patients in the state of Pennsylvania – just trauma patients – found that they had 1,224 different injury related diagnoses in 32,261 combinations.
>
> (Gawande, 2011: 34–35)

Section discussion (CD-ROM)

Predict and prevent is essentially the same as prevention is better than cure. It involves moving the culture of a team or department from reaction to anticipation and intervention. It is about increasing the willingness to intervene in order to minimise the possibility of failure. There are numerous instances of this approach from everyday life. For example, the best way to avoid a heart attack is to stop smoking, not to invest in more cardiac surgeons. And the most effective way to maintain your car's efficiency is to have it regularly serviced.

The surgeon Atul Gawande, author of *The Checklist Manifesto* (2011), was concerned that so many of his patients seemed to suffer serious complications or die unexpectedly in the days after their operation. His analysis led to the conclusion that many of these problems were caused by operating staff failing to follow basic procedures. For example, a surgeon failing to wash his hands properly could cause an infection, or failing to account for all the swabs used in the process could lead to one being left in the patient's body.

Gawande developed a 19-point checklist to be read out before and during each operation to ensure that all of the simple but essential procedures were followed. The outcome was a marked decrease in the number of patients becoming seriously ill or dying after surgery. Checklists are found in many areas of business activity: they are a key tool for airline pilots and those responsible for the preparation of food; manufacturing businesses have standard operating procedures that define the correct way to carry out critical processes; and schools, of course, have lesson plans and assessment criteria.

In his book, Gawande makes the distinction between errors of ignorance (mistakes we make because we don't know enough) and errors of ineptitude (mistakes we make because we don't make proper use of what we know). He suggests that failure in the modern world is usually due to the second of these errors, and he describes how the routine tasks of surgeons have now become so incredibly complicated that mistakes of one kind or another are virtually inevitable. It's just too easy for an otherwise competent doctor to miss a step, forget to ask a vital question or, in the stress and pressure of the moment, fail to plan properly for every eventuality. This is exactly the point about effective management – however inspirational the leadership of a surgeon, hands must be washed and swabs counted!

What implications does this have for the work of your leadership team? Use resource E2(i) to identify some mistakes from the last year in your school (if you claim to have none then we don't believe you!). For each one consider if the error behind it was one of ignorance or ineptitude. The honesty needed for this process is great, but the potential for improvement is even greater.

The best way to close the gap in our schools is to prevent children failing and that means actively challenging poor and inappropriate performance, and that, in turn, means identifying, defining and embedding appropriate performance. While there is a range of strategies and techniques that can help to manage the problem of variation, it is important that such interventions are reinforced and corroborated by a culture of prevention. In other words, it is not just what we do, it is the way that things are done.

E2

All schools are familiar with these principles. Every classroom has instructions about what to do in case of a fire and these are regularly practised. All schools have very clear protocols regarding the management of visitors to the school and safeguarding issues. Virtually every school will have guidelines with regard to pupil behaviour. Yet, many schools do not always have comparable guidelines informing effective teaching and learning.

Look at the checklist in E2(ii) – how might you develop it in order to ensure that all matters relating to effective teaching and learning are being addressed consistently by the leadership team? For every point in the checklist, each member of the team should award a score of 1–10. Then, as a team, identify areas that you wish to improve, and then prioritise your actions.

Key questions

What are the implications for school leaders of Gawande's argument about the importance of specification in order to ensure consistent best practice?

What examples are there in your school of preventative strategies based on the checklist approach? Are they working? If not, why not?

What issues do you need to address in order to eliminate variation but still recognise and celebrate variety?

What can be done to prevent children failing?

Resources (CD-ROM)

| E2(i) | Thinking about mistakes |
| E2(ii) | Effective leadership checklist |

3   More for less – making tough decisions

Question

With unlimited money you can do unlimited things. When money is limited, how do you choose where to spend it?

Why is this important?

The 2008 world financial crisis and ever raising expectations has created a climate where school leaders are faced with unenviable decisions. What is more important, the free breakfast club or the set of new textbooks?

Key quotes for the section

> Doing something isn't always better than doing nothing.
>
> **(Steve Denning)**

> Don't use a lot where a little will do.
>
> **(Proverb)**

> You can't make decisions based on fear and the possibility of what might happen.
>
> **(Michelle Obama)**

Section discussion (CD-ROM)

Every day is full of decisions for the school leader. Some are no-brainers ('Head teacher, would you thank Mrs Smiley for always going the extra mile for the kids'), while many are considerably more challenging ('I strongly suggest you don't replace the teaching assistant but instead buy Learno v4.0 software for all our pupils'). Almost every decision will have both a budgetary and a pupil improvement component; if they don't then they usually make themselves. For example, if there is no resource or budget implication, just a hint of supporting pupil engagement/development will swing the argument for you; whereas a decision with no link to pupil benefit but incurring great cost would be in the realms of insanity ('It is with regret we reject the plan for a Jacuzzi in your office').

Faced with difficult problems there is a continuum of approach from 'the data holds all the answers' to 'my gut says this is what we should do'. Both have their supporters, but the most effective leadership teams place the decision at the centre of a process that uses data, research and intuition to explore possible solutions. To ignore data because it doesn't suit your beliefs is a dangerous route; but, equally, to allow data to lead you in a direction counter to your ethos is unwise. Margaret Spellings (2005), the former US secretary of state, informed her school leaders: 'I often say that what gets measured, gets done. Once we know the contours of the problem, and who is affected, we can put forward a solution.' The problem with this argument is that if it isn't measured, it isn't done – for example, if the mental health of young people is not monitored, you could make a decision that improves pupil attainment but severely effects their well-being.

Some leaders have an aversion to data. During a recent interview process for a new head teacher there was a 50:50 split on the answer to, 'Can a school ever have too much data?' The reasons given by candidates worrying about the volume of data were connected to the fact that many staff are focusing on the numbers rather than on the pupil themselves, and that too many decisions are being driven by particular parts of this data.

So, how does an effective leadership team get the balance right? A good starting point is to ask your budget leader to compile a list of the school's top 20 expenditure lines, and then place them in resource E3(i). Cut up this list into separate boxes and then, as a group, place them in order of their influence on pupil success (where possible use data to assist this process). This is essentially an exercise in cost–benefit analysis, where the benefit is the impact your choices make on the learning and progress of every pupil.

Record your rankings and identify any anomalies. For example, if your biggest expenditure lines are not having the greatest impact on student learning, then investigate the reason for this and consider if there is any way of reducing the amount you spend on this, or alternatively if there is something that you can do to increase its impact.

Now look at the problem with another filter, such as what does the research and/or data suggest are the major strategies that can improve pupil success? Use E3(ii) to gather your top five. For each strategy, identify hazards, reliability of the evidence, costs, implementation time and suitability for your school. If you require stimulus to aid your discussion, the Sutton Trust-Education Endowment Foundation Toolkit (see E1) compares impact with cost for a variety of strategies and will act as a provocation to debate.

Once you have isolated the decisions you wish to make, you must define them in the simplest terms possible. (This may seem like an obvious step, but it is one of the biggest barriers to schools making decisions – lack of clarity about the question will always result in indecision.) Once the issue is defined, make sure you give it the time it deserves – trying to solve your school's major problems in the 10 minutes before everyone rushes to the car park is hardly likely to give you the robust outcome you require. If the decision seems a foregone conclusion, either you have to ask yourself why you haven't done it before or you may be risking a 'lemming mentality' ('Everyone else seems to think this is a good idea – so I guess I do too!'). Good practice would be to allocate at least two members of the team to oppose the issue robustly, regardless of their own views. Strong debate around the issue is the single most important step.

Key questions

Are you being asked to achieve more for less?

If so, are you currently spending your budget well?

Can you improve the effectiveness of any aspect of your work?

Do you need to get rid of something?

Can you define the issue?

Resources (CD-ROM)

| E3(i) | Cost to impact comparison |
| E3(ii) | New strategies: effectiveness and reliability |

4 The school as a social resource

Question

To what extent is the school a public space with its resources available to the wider community?

Why is this important?

Schools that operate a typical pupil day of about 6.5 hours for 190 days a year are functioning for about 16% of the year. This is potentially worrying as in most communities the school represents the single biggest investment of public money and, crucially, its success depends to a very large extent on the quality of its relationships with the community it serves. For very proper reasons, schools are extremely concerned about the safety of their pupils, but this has led to a range of strategies that, in some contexts, might be seen as isolating the school from its environment.

Key quotes for the section

> All uses of a school building, whether during the day, or in the evening, weekend or holiday periods, need to major on security, easy access to the provision of appropriate facilities and easily implemented systems to minimize costs. However, without the strongest community aware ethos, such matters are not at the front of the mind of senior staff and governors.
>
> In addition to potential conflict over priorities in building design at local level, there is considerable potential for further conflict in the management of new and refurbished buildings if the designs do not take account of the needs and requirements of the different stakeholders ... It takes a strong ethos of outreach and community engagement combined with effective liaison and partnership working, to overcome the disadvantages as these 'daytime' staff seek to personalize and 'own' their work areas.
>
> **(Groves, 2008: 105)**

> Schools are at the heart of local communities.
>
> They are places where children become equipped for their future role in society. Many schools have already experienced significant benefits as a result of partnerships based around sharing their facilities which can include educational, economic and broader community benefits that flow from such partnerships.
>
> **(Department of Education, Northern Ireland, n.d.: 4)**

Section discussion (CD-ROM)

There is a bewildering range of relationships between schools and their communities. In some instances, the school is an island with only marginal engagement with the wider community. In other cases, the school is the vibrant heart of its community and provides education in the widest sense of the word. Sometimes the school exists in an essentially reactive mode, responding to external imperatives only when necessary. In other circumstances, the school is the cornerstone of social change and improvement and sees its role as being primarily concerned with every dimension of the variables affecting children's well-being – that is, securing the optimal circumstances for every aspect of a child's life.

As a leadership team, how often do you take time to consider your school's position in the community? With the daily pressures of school life, it is easy for a leadership team to focus on the misbehaviour of little Jimmy or the practicalities of the dinner queue rather than the bigger picture. Why not allocate a large portion of your next meeting to advancing your work with the community? Hand out resource E4(i) in advance and request that every member of the leadership team brings a completed copy to the meeting. Use this as the basis for developing an agreed goal for your work over the coming year, making sure that you are driving the agenda rather than merely responding to it.

The importance of pre-emptive interventions (predicting and preventing) is well understood, especially for younger children. Effective parenting within secure communities is one of the most powerful forces to support well-being and thus educational success and attainment. There are also pragmatic reasons for building stronger relationships between schools and their communities. In a market driven environment, the viability of the school depends partly on the extent to which the community perceive it as 'ours'. It is a well-established principle that schools that are 'owned' by their communities are rarely vandalised. When many school leaders look at the possible benefits of supporting a range of imaginative uses of their premises, they will outweigh these positives with the problems of logistics and cost. However, when you widen the benefits to include increased adult education, improved understanding of modern schooling and better community health, the balance is surely tipped towards increasing the use of the school and its resources.

Use E4(ii) with your leadership team to identify new uses for the school for the benefit of the wider community. The broad sections and examples are meant as a prompt to your discussions, not as an exhaustive list. At this initial stage, the more ideas the better. Don't be tempted to think in terms of practicalities (yet), and don't limit the idea pool to your immediate team – involve the whole staff, the pupils, parents and governors. Remember, your role as a community leader is not to do all the work yourself but to help provide the energy and self-belief for others.

Key questions

How would you react to a university extension studies lecturer who complained that he was unable to get access to the classroom he had been allocated for an evening session as the site manager denied all knowledge of the booking, and when he got to the classroom he found a note from the teacher saying, 'Please leave my classroom as you find it'?

To what extent is your school 'in the community' or 'of the community'?

What evidence is there of the school's commitment to the life of the pupils beyond the classroom?

Is your business manager encouraged to develop alternative uses for school resources?

Who owns your school?

Resources (CD-ROM)

| E4(i) | Your place in the community |
| E4(ii) | Extending the use of school resources |

5   Making a development plan real

Question

How can a development plan become a key part of how your school develops?

Why is this important?

Every school produces a development plan, but how many of these are truly effective? What proportion play a central part in the everyday growth of the school compared with those that sit on a shelf gathering dust until the next inspection?

Key quotes for the section

> Planning is bringing the future into the present so that you can do something about it now.
>
> **(Alan Lakein)**

> Let our advance worrying become advance thinking and planning.
>
> **(Anonymous)**

Section discussion (CD-ROM)

Most of us have heard the proverb, 'failing to plan is planning to fail'. This trite expression will cause most of you to roll your eyes, probably yawn and contemplate looking at another page. The reason for this is that many of us have seen more development plans than Christmases, and yet, if we are honest, few of them have brought about the change that their production hours deserve. So we need to ask ourselves why we are producing them. Ask the rest of your leadership team the same question. A worrying number will no doubt answer 'Ofsted', 'local authority/sponsors' or 'because we've been told to', and this is at the heart of the problem. School leaders are, by the nature of the job, extraordinarily busy, being pulled in many directions by a myriad of tasks, and so will naturally resent working on something which appears to be an administrative task. The reality is, however, that development planning can be at the heart of your school's progress, but you have to want it to be.

A major issue, one that is much more than a semantic debate, is whether your planning process results in a *development* plan or an *improvement* plan. Is your planning process simply a way of allocating the budget and prioritising resourcing decisions, or is it part of a strategic and cumulative improvement process that is designed to embed aspects of your school's preferred future scenario (see B3)?

The first major step is to decide who the plan is for; if it is designed solely for an external audience then success is unlikely. Consider how the plan can be made to benefit a wider audience, not just staff and governors, but pupils and parents as well. Imagine the power of a development plan that directly involves pupils in the improvement of their own school. So, to summarise, the success of the plan is as much about how you do it as what is actually in it.

To help get you started, here are five steps for developing a successful plan:

1 *Build awareness of the importance of a school improvement plan – why is it important?* Think of this as a PR exercise. By increasing the enthusiasm for the plan across all areas of the school you will automatically increase its effectiveness. We are not suggesting 'Hug a development plan' posters on every wall, but the use of positive language whenever it is mentioned will help. Saying, 'I'm afraid we've been told we've got to do one of those boring development plan thingies,' is not the way to begin!

2 *Quality assurance – how are we doing?* What is the health of the school? Have you a good handle on how things are progressing on a wide range of fronts? Data? Observations? Parental feedback? Have you carried out a systematic survey of pupil attitudes to learning?

3 *Identify what you need to change.* Have you identified the areas in need of work? If not, use the strategies in E1.

4 *Writing the plan – how will we make the changes?* The first question is, who are you going to involve in drawing up the plan? Teaching staff? Support staff? Governors? Pupils? Parents? The second question is, do you really mean 'involve'? True engagement will require joint planning, debate, construction and, eventually, monitoring. Simply showing the development plan to your stakeholders does not constitute involvement. You then need to decide the design of plan you are going to use. Resources E5(i–iii) are different styles of plan, but we strongly advise schools to adapt and find a system that suits them.

5 *Frequently monitor and evaluate the plan.* Be prepared to refine it as needed. We have worked as part of leadership teams where we started with the very best of intentions to keep our plan central to our meetings, but then lunchtime duty rotas, arrangements for parents' evening, marauding ducks or whatever else grabbed our attention would

get in the way. The plan must be made so important that it doesn't get shifted down the agenda – and if something else is so important, why isn't it on the plan?

So, treat your plan like your lover: spend time with it (frequently), respect it, think about it constantly, talk about it to others and, if it isn't working, don't be afraid to change it!

Key questions

Why do you want a plan? Do you really, really want a plan?

Is your planning about incremental adjustment or a shared improvement process?

How do you raise its importance with others?

Who do you involve in its construction?

How do you keep it in the minds of the senior leadership team?

Resources (CD-ROM)

E5(i)	School improvement plan
E5(ii)	School improvement plan (academic year)
E5(iii)	School improvement plan (key issues)

Leading people

1   The school as a community

Question

In order to maximise school effectiveness, do we need to spend as much time on the social aspects of the school as on aspects of teaching and learning?

Why is this important?

There is a very close link between organisational structure and organisational culture. How an activity is structured has a significant impact on performance, relationships and the capacity to improve and develop. The crucial principle here is the notion that form follows function – the essential criterion for effective design. If the core purpose or function of a school is the successful learning of every pupil, then what does this tell us about the way that schools need to be structured and the culture created and sustained?

Key quotes for the section

> We don't come fully formed into the world. We learn how to think, how to walk, how to speak, how to behave, indeed how to be human from other human beings. We need other human beings in order to be human. We are made for togetherness ... to exist in a tender network of interdependence ... That is how you have Ubuntu [I am because we are] – you care, you are hospitable, you're gentle, you're compassionate and concerned.
>
> **(Archbishop Desmond Tutu, quoted in Battle, 2009: 54)**

> At present, the tragedy of school change is that only about 30 per cent of the explanation for variations in school achievement appears to be attributable to factors in the school ... Perhaps it is now time for leaders to lead their schools and exert their influence far beyond the school walls.
>
> **(Moreno et al., 2006: 5)**

F1

Section discussion (CD-ROM)

There seems little doubt that living in a community is good news. If we live in effective communities, then we live longer, we are less likely to become ill and more likely to recover from illness, we are less likely to be the victim of crime and less likely to become a criminal. More importantly, perhaps, our children are likely to have a better sense of well-being, higher levels of academic success and significantly improved life chances if they grow up in effective families in successful communities.

Before focusing on the community within our schools, it might be useful to think about the factors that apply in all situations. The quality of community life is often expressed in terms of social capital. A successful community will have high social capital to the extent that it meets most of the following criteria:

→ It operates through consent and consensus around explicit values and clear norms.

→ It works through highly sophisticated communication with a shared vocabulary and rules of grammar, using modern technologies and traditional social and relational skills.

→ There is a high degree of mutual trust, regard and friendship.

→ It is self-managing and self-organising and develops strategies and protocols to support its working processes. People are involved in the politics of the community; they stand for office, vote in elections and contribute to public debate.

→ There are signs, symbols and rituals to express and reinforce a sense of community identity; the community comes together to celebrate its shared identity.

→ Relationships are characterised in terms of interdependence and reciprocity; people care for each other and accept mutual responsibility.

→ Much of the life of the community is expressed through volunteering and working for the common good through collaborative projects.

→ The overall sense of the community is one of hope and aspiration; there is a strong sense of a positive collective future.

→ The community values learning and seeks out those who represent the accumulated wisdom of the community.

This provides a demanding list for any school. For many leaders, the school community has been a by-product of their actions rather than the focus of their strategy. Making the effectiveness of the wider community your focus will introduce new priorities to the way you work. As a team, use resource F1(i) as a starting point for analysing your current work, and then use the same criteria in F1(ii) to identify areas of possible work. Do not limit your thoughts by trying to produce quick wins – start with quantity before applying the filter of quality!

The interesting and challenging issue that emerges from this work on community is twofold. First, should we work towards the notion of developing the school as a community – in other words, should the school become a microcosm of the wider community in order to ensure that every learner has the experience of living and working in an authentic community? The second, and closely related, issue is the challenge for the school to go beyond its boundaries and to become an agency for developing social capital in the wider community.

Start this discussion with your governing body. What is their vision for your learning community. Do they believe that you have the correct balance between organisation and community? F1(iii) provides a mechanism for investigating the continuum within your school – complete this with as wide a variety of participants as possible and then analyse your results. Are you happy that the school is getting the balance right?

Key questions

Does your personal and professional experience confirm or deny the claims made in this section for the importance of community?

How would you characterise the community your school serves?

What evidence would you offer to describe the relationship between educational success and effective community?

Is your school a community in microcosm?

What, for you, are the major differences between leading a school as an organisation and leading a learning community?

F1

Resources (CD-ROM)

F1(i)	The school as a community (what you currently do)
F1(ii)	The school as a community (what you might do)
F1(iii)	The continuum between organisation and community

2   Leading through trust

Question

Is trust an important component of a successful school?

Why is this important?

If trust is important in leadership then we need to understand why this is so. We also need to be able to recognise how it develops and how to measure if our leadership affects it.

Key quotes for the section

> To be persuasive, we must be believable; to be believable, we must be credible; to be credible, we must be truthful.
>
> **(Edward R. Murrow)**

> Your reputation and integrity are everything. Follow through on what you say you're going to do. Your credibility can only be built over time, and it is built from the history of your words and actions.
>
> **(Maria Razumich-Zec)**

> It's a vice to trust everyone, and equally a vice to trust no one.
>
> **(Seneca)**

Section discussion (CD-ROM)

Have you ever resorted to the phrase, 'Trust me, I'm a … (insert job title to fit)'? If so, you will have realised how hollow the words sound. You cannot be forced to trust another person; trust is internally generated, not externally imposed.

First, let's consider if trust is really something we need to worry about – in these days of e-learning and benchmarking, surely a good system is all we need? While many leaders may not have creating trust in the workplace as one of their priorities, we have yet to meet one who claims, 'Mistrust and fear, that's what creates a great school!' In their research into high performing elementary schools in Chicago, Bryk and Schneider (2002) found a high correlation between the levels of trust in a school and its capacity to improve. Schools with a high level of trust at the outset of a programme to improve maths and reading had a one in two chance of improving. Schools with relatively low levels of trust had only a one in seven chance of improving. Schools in the latter category that did improve made significant gains in their levels of trust as a prerequisite to raising attainment.

Bryk et al. (2010: 45–46) report on a detailed and systematic longitudinal study carried out since 1989 looking at over 100 schools that have improved, compared with over 100 schools that have declined. The key differences between the schools has enabled them to create a framework for school improvement that is made up of a number of 'essential supports':

1   Leadership as the driver for change.

2   Parent–community ties.

3   Professional capacity – promoting the quality of staff and focusing on improvement.

4   A student-centred learning climate.

5   Instructional guidance – focusing on ambitious educational achievement for every child.

Bryk et al. see these components as akin to the recipe for a cake. But just as putting the ingredients for a cake into a bowl is not enough to make a cake:

> [T]hen trust represents the social energy, or the 'oven's heat,' necessary for transforming these basic ingredients into comprehensive school change. Absent the social energy provided by trust, improvement initiatives are unlikely to culminate in meaningful change, regardless of their intrinsic merit.
>
> **(Bryk et al., 2010: 157)**

This is where so much of our current system fails. It is too politically driven, resulting in an unhealthy focus on the ingredients rather than the method. 'Experts' see a wonderful cake, one that is superb in look, smell and taste, and then become obsessed about its constituents. Identical ingredients can, and will, be turned into a revolting mush without due care.

For the five strategies listed above to be successful they need to be set in a climate of trust, so the question becomes, how do leaders create a climate of trust? This appears to be a conundrum when those same leaders may need to make many difficult decisions. However, not dealing with problems is no route to developing trust either; the key is to focus on forming respectful relationships at all levels. Respect, and in turn trust, is formed when there is an openness surrounding decision making, when problems for the school are widened beyond a small team and alternative perspectives are sought. The decision may still need to be made by the leader, but even when the decision is unpopular trust will not be damaged.

The first step to improving levels of trust in your school would be to evaluate current levels. This could be done by issuing a simple survey (e.g. F2(i)) for pupils, parents, staff, leaders and governors) and then tabulating the results in a simple way (e.g. F2(ii)) to compare results and identify any issues.

When you have identified areas where trust is weak (e.g. staff view of leaders), share the results of the survey, and, more importantly, what you intend to do about it – words alone will do nothing. Decide on a series of actions and repeat the survey to see if it works. Trust us, it will!

Key questions

Do you want to develop trust in your school? Why?

Do you have an understanding of how others judge levels of trust in your school?

Can you identify anything that is destroying trust?

Can you create a plan to improve levels of trust?

Resources (CD-ROM)

F2(i)	Trust survey
F2(ii)	Trust survey results

3 Challenging conversations

Question

When are challenging conversations with leaders justified, and what are the principles informing their usage?

Why is this important?

With the best will in the world, there will be times when leaders need to challenge the poor performance or inappropriate behaviour of colleagues. Hopefully, the challenging conversation is the exception rather than the rule, and a range of alternative strategies will have been explored before the need to resort to extremes.

It is important at the outset to stress that, for most purposes in education, the use of challenge is not a negative – for example, it is a crucial element in effective feedback and is fundamental to any model of intelligent accountability. However, in terms of the effective leadership of staff, the need to question and challenge aspects of colleagues' work is usually quite rare.

Key quotes for the section

> There are two choices for staff who are not up to it: they leave or they stay. If they leave then there are two styles of departure – by agreement and with a blessing or through the competency procedures. If they stay then they either accept the need to improve or they don't. If they accept then it's knuckle down and agree a development plan.
>
> In either of these scenarios it is vital to retain objectivity, separate the person from their behaviours and focus on facts. It's an emotional drain to argue over differences of opinion so focus on facts.
>
> **(Smith, 2011: 165)**

> Yet what we're dealing with is *human stuff*, just human stuff – thoughts, emotions, sensations in the body, physiology, ideas, beliefs, memories, and imaginations. And within all of that stuff is just frames. There's nothing more. That's why there's nothing to fear. There's no aliens or demons inside. There's just strong, intense thoughts and emotions. And because it is all *human*, you can fully accept and embrace it and explore it, can you not?
>
> **(Hall, 2003: 226)**

Section discussion (CD-ROM)

Leaders intervene to address staff performance across a wide spectrum of difficult, challenging and inappropriate behaviours that extend from the illegal/criminal to the mildly irritating. Certain behaviours, such as criminal activity involving acts of violence, theft, fraud or gross professional misconduct, are covered by very formal, legally determined procedures. Others are less clear and the issue is one of relative perception and impact. An analysis of the possible types of behaviour that could be regarded as difficult cover a very broad range – with the obvious implication that they require an appropriate level and style of response. These include:

→ Racist, sexist and inappropriate political attitudes.

→ Behaviour in breach of contract (e.g. absenteeism, habitual lateness).

→ Incompetence.

→ Poor performance.

→ Failure to implement improvement.

→ Negativity and non-cooperation.

→ Lack of engagement and commitment.

→ Failure to implement agreed policies.

→ Obstructive attitude at meetings.

→ Anti-social and withdrawn behaviour.

Apart from the obvious legal and contractual issues, different types of poor behaviour call for a range of different responses appropriate to the seriousness of the misdemeanour. Equally, it has to be remembered that most problems involving poor performance, inappropriate behaviour or failure to fully engage will almost always have emotional roots. The response to such behaviour will also be emotional, and this is where emotional intelligence in leadership is so important. However fraught the process, leaders must retain a difficult balance of objectivity and empathy while also remaining focused on the core issues. While the dignity of a colleague is important, so is the quality of their work. In the final analysis, children do not have the time to lose while adults sort out their professional relationship problems.

So, once the problem has been identified, what is the best course for action? Ideally, problems of poor performance and/or inappropriate professional behaviour should be pre-empted by a school's culture. A positive culture that develops a sense of shared commitment to high performance and levels of professional engagement

F3

should prevent some of these problems from occurring in the first place. If they do, however, leaders should be focused on securing commitment through moral consensus and high expectations, which can often be the most powerful antidote to poor or inappropriate performance.

Inevitably, prevention, working through consensus and peer pressure will not always work. At the very outset of any strategy, it is vital that you understand your own motivation and that you monitor your personal and professional responses – your coach (and if you don't have one – why not?) or a senior member of staff should help you to clarify the most appropriate approaches. Long before moving towards a capability procedure, you may need to change the nature of your interaction with a colleague because of their behaviour or attitudes (rather than their professional competence).

Challenging conversations need to be very formal as they might well, in time, be the subject of legal scrutiny and the basis of appeals or legal claims. Here are some suggestions for keeping it formal:

→ Clarify the nature and status of the meeting – why is the meeting necessary?

→ Place the issue in context and recognise and reinforce the positive contributions that have been made.

→ Raise your concerns in a precise, clear, logical and non-emotive way.

→ Listen very carefully to your colleague's point of view and respond with empathy.

→ Ensure that every concern is backed up by appropriate evidence and reference to school policies, requirements and standards.

→ Try to secure agreement about the implications of the problem behaviour.

→ Avoid threat, but challenge and invite responses, explanations and interpretations.

→ Reinforce and restate your central concerns.

→ Remain objective and dispassionate.

→ Terminate the discussion if it becomes emotional or personally abusive.

→ Record all details.

→ If possible, agree future performance standards (e.g. attendance and behaviour at meetings, use of assessment policies).

→ Return the relationship to a normal professional performance management approach as soon as possible.

→ Monitor performance and intervene if necessary; equally, reinforce and consolidate improvement.

→ Use a senior member of staff, or your coach, to support you through the process.

Resource F3(i) has been produced as a template for using the stages outlined above. You might find this useful as a way of ensuring that the meeting is productive and remains focused. A balance needs to be struck between the member of staff not feeling threatened and them not realising that the issue is important. (There are examples of teachers being 'spoken to' who remain blissfully unaware that there is a problem!) Ensure that there is a clear agreement of the outcomes of the discussion. Resource F3(ii) is a template for the agreement statement – the language has been kept deliberately neutral to ensure the focus is on the outcome and not the process.

This process can be handled in a variety of ways. However, if you think some of your colleagues might not handle situations like these with the required sensitivity (perhaps they do not always display strong emotional intelligence), discuss potential issues at an early stage among the team and agree on the 'right' way of handling any problems that could arise.

Key questions

How do you respond emotionally to the prospect of a challenging conversation with a colleague?

A major cause of poor performance is a lack of clear definitions and expectations ('If you don't tell me what you want, you deserve what you get'). How clear are your expectations?

Do all members of the leadership team accept the need to hold all staff accountable for their performance, and are they confident in doing so?

How consistent is performance management across the school?

How emotionally literate are senior staff?

F3

Resources (CD-ROM)

F3(i)	Important discussions pro forma
F3(ii)	Record of professional conversation

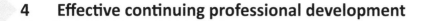

4   Effective continuing professional development

Question

Do we know how effective our staff training programmes are, and can we identify how to improve them?

Why is this important?

With many schools showing five figure staff development budgets, it is vital that we are able to assess if training is having an effect worthy of the expenditure. Then, more importantly, leaders need to pinpoint strategies that will increase its effectiveness.

Key quotes for the section

> It has long been known that the most powerful influences on teachers are other teachers, but policies have rarely built on the fact. The best way of exploiting this phenomenon is through regular, face-to-face encounters among professionals that focus on the improvement of teaching and learning.
>
> **(Hargreaves, 2010: 23)**

> The future is already here – it's just not very evenly distributed.
>
> **(William Gibson)**

> Lord, if I die, I hope it's during in-service training, because the transition to death would be so subtle.
>
> **(poster)**

Section discussion (CD-ROM)

One thing we can be sure of is that spending huge amounts on training will not always be money well spent. The question of quality and effectiveness must always be considered alongside price.

The standard model of teacher training developed over the past 50 years has been fundamentally a top down one. This was honed to a fine art in the National Strategies of the 1990s when a pyramid, or cascade, model was used: a team of trainers was sent out into the world and each of them trained more teachers, who, in turn, trained the staff in their own school. To ensure a consistent message, it became a very formalised process and, consequently, very impersonal and sanitised. It also had the effect of producing a generation of teachers who believed that information must come from above. Many teachers now turn to external providers to bring in new ideas as their default approach, rather than beginning by developing their support from within. We write this as two people who are regularly asked to deliver training, and while we don't want to bite the hands that feed us, we would ask that you really make sure you need us! Externally delivered information can often be entertaining and challenging, but if the outcome is a short lived 'feel good' factor, then surely there are better ways to spend your money.

So, what type of training would work for your school? We would like to propose an approach which is referred to as JPD (joint practice development) rather than CPD (continuing professional development). The key differences between CPD and JPD are that CPD is driven from an external source, with a process managed by school leaders and often with a generic content, whereas JPD is a more leader facilitated process, often focused on a particular issue relevant to the school. (Use resource F4(i) to analyse your training provision over the past year and then identify ways to improve the balance.) Various teaching union campaigns over the past few years have called for teachers to work to rule – that is, to only work the hours for which they are contracted (the dreaded 1,265 hours debate, an arbitrary figure introduced by Education Secretary Kenneth Baker in the late 1980s). During these disputes, many teachers sit in meetings or training sessions watching the clock, waiting for the moment when the agreed time passed and then walking out. How tragic is this? Who is being hurt? If the training had been planned by the teachers, and was perceived as relevant and valuable, would teachers so readily use it as a tool to fight the government? (A clear case of biting off your nose to spite your face.) If, however, training is imposed and it is tedious and lacks relevance, most people will use any reason to avoid it. JPD makes sense on every level.

If you want to improve the training in your school, the research summary in resource F4(ii) is a good place to start. Consider the effect sizes of a variety of actions. Most leaders do not intuitively expect these results. The message is clear: in an age when many schools are adopting a regimented, almost authoritarian approach to in-service training, the effects of resourcing or providing a target driven approach pale into insignificance when compared with you, the leaders, actually participating in the training and its preparation. So, no more introducing the speaker and then going to do 'something more important'. There is nothing more important than you being part of the training and learning with your colleagues.

So, if you are serious about making a difference, form a training group and give it power and money. Be part of the training group, but also make sure as wide a group of staff are involved as possible. Agree as a group what your training needs are (don't bring a list from the latest Ofsted report), and make the work of this group the most important part of your job.

Key questions

What is training for?

Who is it for?

Are you paying for external training? If so, do you use the potential of your own staff to the full?

When you do pay, how do you make sure the learning is across the whole school?

Do you have CPD or JPD? Which one do you want?

Resources (CD-ROM)

| F4(i) | CPD vs. JPD |
| F4(ii) | Professional learning |

5   Shared leadership

Question

Is leadership about the personal status of a few individuals or the collective capacity of the school?

Why is this important?

British culture tends to categorise leadership in hierarchical terms. Leaders are seen as people with personal and positional power – individuals who have status and privileges commensurate with their role. When he was prime minister, Winston Churchill wished for the same power as the headmaster of an English public school. There is no doubt that head teachers are different. They are able to exercise significant power and authority, but they are also highly personally accountable. In many ways, English head teachers are among the most personally accountable professionals in society.

For a number of reasons, there has been a significant questioning of the historic model of school leadership and a movement towards shared or distributed leadership – moving from a hierarchical structure to a much flatter organisation. The pivotal issue is the extent to which authority and responsibility are shared.

Key quotes for the section

> [A]n ultimate goal of sustainable learning and leadership is that, in time, the vast majority of schools will become authentic and assertive professional learning communities that will constitute the strong cells of system wide improvement. Ultimately, leadership that stays centered on learning and that lasts over time is deliberately distributed leadership that stretches across a school or system, is a genuinely shared responsibility, and is taken as much as given.
>
> **(Hargreaves and Fink, 2006: 139)**

> The most significant results of this study for our purposes, however, were the indirect effects of total leadership on student learning and achievement, through its direct effects on the three dimensions of staff performance. Total leadership accounted for a quite significant 27 per cent of the variation in student achievement across schools. This is a much higher proportion of explained variation (two to three times higher) than is typically reported in studies of individual headteacher effects.
>
> **(Leithwood et al., 2006: 12)**

Section discussion (CD-ROM)

The discussion about shared leadership starts with a semantic issue – is it shared or distributed? Shared leadership tends to imply that leadership is a collective activity which is available to all. Distributed leadership suggests that leadership is essentially the property of, or in the gift of, the head teacher. In a military context or in large hierarchies, like the civil service or commercial corporations, leadership is generally distributed. It is often closely linked to a career structure, promotion, access to the control of resources and the ability to make significant choices.

There is little doubt that some schools do embody some aspects of the distributed leadership model – it might, for example, be a function of size and complexity. However, there is a case for arguing that hierarchical leadership is not at all appropriate for schools for a variety of reasons. These include:

→ Teachers are professionals – they should work in a professional community based on parity of esteem and mutual respect, not a bureaucratic hierarchy.

→ School leadership is too complex and demanding for one person – the development of the school leadership team points to significant advantages in terms of effective group working.

→ Schools need to be seen as learning communities working through interdependent, collaborative relationships involving all the adults and pupils.

→ School structures need to be flexible in order to recognise and reinforce ability and talent – the ability to lead is neither genetic nor age related.

The key determinant of shared leadership is the relationship between authority and responsibility. How much responsibility does an individual have, and do they have the commensurate authority to go with that level of responsibility? Our careers often reflect a growth in responsibility and authority, but they are often not in balance – that is, responsibility without appropriate authority means that the individual is constantly having to seek permission. Although running the risk of offending schools who are proudly claiming their authoritarian badge (and there are some!), we would characterise the continuum as one of 'maturing' leadership. There are four main levels of growth: control, delegation, empowerment and subsidiarity.

1   Control is exemplified when one person is responsible for all decision making, when power and authority are exercised without consultation and when individuals carry out orders. It usually serves to create dependency, passivity and alienation.

F5

2   Delegation is how most organisations work. Individuals are given limited amounts of authority and responsibility within highly defined levels of tasks and outcomes.

3   Empowerment means that high levels of authority are devolved. What has to be done is usually defined, but how it is done is left to those who have the responsibility. This implies control over resources, methods and decision making.

4   Subsidiarity means that power is fully distributed across the organisation. Just as in a federal state (like Germany or Australia), a wide range of powers are discharged at a 'local' level without reference to the centre.

Use resource F5(i) to begin analysing the leadership within your own school. As a team, look at the continuum of characteristics described above the table, marking the points on the arrows that best describe your current situation. Decide from this which category of leadership best describes your school.

This model can be used to describe the working structure of the school, but it also applies to the classroom and all learning situations. In some classrooms pupils have genuine authority to exercise real choices; in others there is a dependent relationship with the teacher. It is worth reflecting on the most appropriate structure to support effective learning. Use F5(ii) to categorise classes within your school. If your analysis shows a great variety of classification within the school, consider the effect this will have on pupils. If you categorise yourself as a school of empowerment, are you prepared to accept some of your classrooms will have a control culture?

A central principle of effective design is that form follows function – for example, a sports car and a family saloon are very different in design (form) because they have very different functions. Is your leadership designed for purpose? If not, what steps are you able to take that will encourage it on the path to maturity?

Key questions

Is your school leadership structure fit for purpose (i.e. does it work)?

Where is your school on the continuum described in resource F5(ii)? Why is it there, and what are the implications for your leadership?

Are leadership roles in your school dominated by gender, experience and age, or by ability?

How much discretion do pupils, classroom teachers, middle leaders, senior staff and support staff have to make significant decisions?

Does holding a leadership role in your school carry any privileges (e.g. reserved car parking)?

How do you reconcile autonomy and accountability?

Resources (CD-ROM)

F5(i)	Authority and responsibility in your leadership team
F5(ii)	Authority and responsibility in the classroom

Collaboration

1 Reconciling autonomy and collaboration

Question

Which is the more important for a school: to be separate and looking after itself, or to be working as part of a bigger group?

Why is this important?

Schools face the problem of autonomy every day. Current government policy appears to be contradictory. (What, a policy that doesn't make sense? Never!) On one hand it suggests that collaboration is essential, but on the other it adopts practices that pitch schools into competition with each other.

Key quotes for the section

> In the long history of humankind (and animal kind, too) those who learned to collaborate and improvise most effectively have prevailed.
>
> **(Charles Darwin)**

> I think there's great potential for autonomy, but we have to remember that we live in a world where people may have free will but have not invented their circumstances.
>
> **(Thomas Frank)**

> The power of collective capacity is that it enables ordinary people to accomplish extraordinary things – for two reasons. One is that knowledge about effective practice becomes more widely available and accessible on a daily basis. The second reason is more powerful still – working together generates commitment. Moral purpose, when it stares you in the face through students and your peers working together to make lives and society better, is palpable, indeed virtually irresistible.
>
> **(Fullan, 2010: 72)**

G1

> The hardest part of sustainable leadership is the part that provokes us to think beyond our own schools and ourselves. It is the part that calls us to serve the public good of all people's children within and beyond our community and not only the private interests of those who subscribe to our own institution.
>
> **(Hargreaves and Fink, 2006: 158)**

Section discussion (CD-ROM)

There are a number of factors which currently appear to be driving schools towards going it alone. For example, the use of league tables alongside the focus on parental choice will inevitably force schools to look at ways to outshine their nearest neighbours. Results drive pupil numbers, which drive funding, which in turn drives the recruitment of quality teachers. Additionally, most examination boards operate a norm referencing system (only a particular percentage can pass) rather than a criteria referenced one (as long as entrants achieve a given standard any number can pass). This gives holistic educators a problem: for any one child to succeed another must fail. This might lead us to think that the government believes that autonomy is the way forward for our schools. But they don't, or at least they say they don't. Most governments praise collaboration and tell schools this is absolutely the way forward. But they do this without resolving the underlying drivers in favour of autonomy.

When the praised model is one of a 'good school' taking over a 'poor school', collaboration is not always a healthy paradigm. Interestingly, some schools are trying to find a balance between collaboration and autonomy. For example, the website of one group of academies claims that they believe in the concept of 'collaborative autonomy', which on the surface appears to be an oxymoron. However, this is an interesting experiment in adopting the benefits of both autonomy and collaboration but, presumably, trying to avoid the downsides of both.

So, what about you, the keen and dynamic leadership team working on this issue, what is best for your school? First, let's think about autonomy. Do you have everything you need within your own four walls? Complete resource G1(i), initially as individual members of the team, and then gather your results to produce a composite version for the school. Ideally involve governors and the wider staff body at this time. If you are in the position of only having entries in the first column, autonomy is easy for you and there is probably already a queue of schools waiting to join you – or else you aren't taking this process seriously. Most schools will have entries in all columns and will have built up a picture of the areas in which they are strong and those in need of further work. Entries in the competent column (B) are possibilities for collaboration, but may well be ideal for working on within your own school. Entries in the final column (C) are almost certainly an excellent area for collaboration. In true collaborative style, one school will have weaknesses which can be supported by another, while at the same time a reciprocal arrangement in another area is occurring the opposite way.

Once you have identified your areas of need, some real bravery is needed – you need to share your self-analysis with other schools. Once this initial step is taken, give other schools the grid and invite them to be equally honest. If a group of schools is prepared to be this open, genuine collaboration is possible. Use form G1(ii) to collate the results for each potential partner and identify leads for each topic.

It must be emphasised that without considerable amounts of trust, both within and between schools, this, or any other collaboration, will quickly fail.

Key questions

Can the school do it all alone?

What will happen if it does stand alone?

What are the dangers of collaboration?

What are the benefits of collaboration?

In which areas would collaboration be particularly beneficial for your school?

In which areas can you offer help to other schools?

Resources (CD-ROM)

G1(i)	School strengths and weaknesses
G1(ii)	Collaboration results table

2 Strategies for collaborative working

Question

What leadership strategies are most likely to lead to successful and authentic collaboration?

Why is this important?

The movement towards autonomous schools and the self-improving school system has led to an increased focus on the capacity of schools to work collaboratively. And it has become clear that successful collaboration is not a given. Although there are many examples of highly effective partnership working, genuine collaboration is about much more than just being a good neighbour. For very good reasons, not least the accountability model based on the Ofsted inspection, schools operate with a high degree of autonomy, as can the teachers and teams within schools.

There is powerful, if not compelling, evidence that collaborative working is one of the most successful strategies in securing sustainable school improvement. The success of the London Challenge, based largely on collaborative working, is testament to the potential for cooperation. It is equally clear that at a time of increased expectations for schools' performance, the loss of the traditional infrastructure of support and the very real demands for increased efficiency in managing resources point to the need to find new types of relationship between schools.

Key quotes for the section

> In a self-improving school system, more control and responsibility passes to the local level in a spirit of mutual aid between school leaders and their colleagues, who are morally committed to imaginative and sustainable ways of achieving more ambitious and better outcomes.
>
> **(Hargreaves, 2010: 19)**

> Many of the schools in our study engaged in on-field friendly rivalry with their peers to push each others' performance higher, but not in win–lose competitions where some schools would prosper at the expense of others. Leaders who perform beyond expectations practise friendly rivalry, promote co-opetition and possess a collaborative edge.
>
> **(Hargreaves and Harris, 2011: 65)**

Section discussion (CD-ROM)

Successful collaboration requires a range of strategies and skills that are well known but not always available. In most studies of successful cooperation, collaboration and shared approaches, seven areas always emerge:

1   *Shared values.* A clear sense of common purpose built around agreed moral principles seems to be the recipe for almost any school from the smallest primary school to the largest academy chain. Without an explicit set of agreed working principles, it is difficult to see how a collective endeavour stands any chance of working. High performance leadership and high performance schools start with a consensus about the fundamental principles that will inform decision making and choices.

2   *Shared vision, scenarios and strategy.* Once values have been established it becomes possible to build a sense of the future – that is, having agreed on why collaboration is necessary, the next stage is to agree on what difference the collaboration will make. This is probably best done by working on agreed scenarios for the future that essentially 'tell the story' of what difference the collaboration will make.

3   *Shared/democratic leadership.* Collaboration implies the development of interdependent working and that, in turn, implies shared and democratic approaches to leadership. This means that leadership is based on capability rather than perceived status or political significance. It is also essential that leadership reflects the nature of the community that the collaboration is to serve.

4   *Multiple interdependent networks.* Successful collaboration, especially for schools, has to recognise that schools will be involved in multiple networks with differing levels of engagement and commitment. From the legal and contractual nature of chains, federations and trusts, through alliances to partnerships and networks, schools are involved in a complex web of relationships that require skilled leadership.

5   *Participative projects.* It is no surprise that collaborative working develops best through working together. Collaboration means working together on projects that translate values and scenarios into concrete experiences across the community.

6   *Developing relational skills.* Trust is pivotal to collaboration. This points to a sophisticated level of mutual respect and interdependent working.

7   *Open accountability.* As well the formal accountability based on Ofsted criteria, and the rather less well-defined notion of the moral accountability of

the professional, there also needs to be a mutual accountability that underpins the collaborative process. This is an expression of mutual responsibility, interdependence and recognition of the status and significance attached to collaborative working.

Use resource G2(i) to begin looking at your partnerships. A series of questions covering the seven areas identified here will prompt your thinking. Consider all the partners you are working with, or expecting to work with, and investigate the reasons and passions behind your work. It might be useful to attempt to complete an organisational map for your existing partnerships, and then use the map to identify how you would like these to develop. Use G2(ii) as a template, and ensure that you not only depict your school organisation on the map but also the pupils and community that would be affected by this alliance. A partnership that does not focus on the benefit to these groups is not likely to succeed.

Key questions

Before considering collaboration between schools, how effective is the collaboration within your school?

To what extent are the values in any collaboration that you belong to known, shared, understood and, crucially, acted on?

How clear are the long term aspirations of your collaboration?

How would you characterise the leadership of the collaboration?

How complex are the networks and partnerships in which your school participates? Are there tensions in terms of competing priorities or value systems?

What sort of collaborative projects has your school been involved in, and how successful have they been?

What have been the significant relational issues to emerge through collaborative working?

How does accountability work in your collaborative relationships?

Resources (CD-ROM)

G2(i)   Starting to look at partnerships

G2(ii)   An organisational map

G3

3 Sustaining the school while working in the system

Question

How does a school leader look after the welfare of the school while keeping their external audience happy?

Why is this important?

The modern school leader has a demanding position as the link between state and pupil. The pressures come from both sides. The leader tries to keep both sides happy – and is in danger of failing both.

Key quotes for the section

> I don't know whether I am key. Logic dictates that as head you have to be key. Research on organisations say a head is, but I can almost work myself out of a job by creating an environment where others have leadership roles. It's difficult to say one person is more important than others.
>
> **(head teacher quoted in Bolam et al., 2005: 126)**

> An employee's motivation is a direct result of the sum of interactions with his or her manager.
>
> **(Bob Nelson)**

> Employees who believe that management is concerned about them as a whole person – not just an employee – are more productive, more satisfied, more fulfilled.
>
> **(Anne M. Mulcahy)**

Section discussion (CD-ROM)

It sometimes feels like an impossible job to be the buffer between national policy and the immediate day-to-day issues of your staff and pupils. The problem is that if you feel it is impossible, it probably is. Roses may benefit from being overloaded by large heaps of manure, but this is not true for leaders. The dilemma that many leaders face is that the requirements of national government often appear to be in direct opposition to the needs of the organisation. So, what options do leaders have in this position?

1 *Focus the organisation on providing exactly what the government are asking for.*

Benefit: If you achieve the external targets everyone seems to gain – the school (financial reward), the pupils (improved personal achievement), the staff and parents (associated with a 'successful school') and, of course, *you* (arise Dame Deidre!).

Drawback: The journey may take its toll on staff and leaders. It is easy for staff and pupils to lose sight of what education is really for; staff may begin to see the pupils as numbers and pupils to think staff are not interested in them as individuals. When success is achieved, it may appear to be a success for the leaders rather than the school.

2 *Focus the organisation on immediate internal needs.*

Benefit: Staff morale will be high and community needs can become a positive focus. The team spirit will grow and long term plans for incremental change will be developed.

Drawback: A focus on the broader welfare of the organisation may detract from the more immediate goals of government. Organisations can lack drive and become insular and safe.

3 *Do both! Find ways to drive change that involves the staff and pupils as part of the change.*

If this is successful we can have the benefit without the drawbacks; but incorrectly approached it could be the other way round.

One way to approach the problem is to realise that it does not have to be an either/or situation. It may be possible to have both sprints and marathons occurring at the same time. Use resource G3(i) to analyse the needs of your school. Look at the full spectrum of needs, both internal and external, and then select a mixture of short term (sprint) solutions and long term (marathon) activities. If staff are included in this analysis, they will have more opportunity to buy into the process and not believe that it has been imposed.

We should be concerned about leaders who appear to believe that 'passing the kick' is the best way to drive change – that is, in fearing criticism from above they instil a similar (or increased) fear in their own staff. Use the analysis process to identify sprint activities and share these across the school (this is what we are doing and why). Ensure

G3

that marathon activities include ones that are sustaining to both pupils and staff. Ensure that the results of sprints are shared, but that the progress of marathon activities is seen as being just as important.

Key questions

What does the government require from your school?

Would doing this damage the school? How and why?

Can you find activities which support internal and external needs?

Can you split your actions into short term and long term?

Resources (CD-ROM)

G3(i)   Sprint and marathon activities

4   Pupils as partners in learning

Question

To what extent should pupils be active participants in their learning and in the life of their school?

Why is this important?

There is a wide range of opinions on the status of pupils as members of their school community. This breadth tends to reflect attitudes to childhood on a spectrum from the immature dependent to an autonomous person with rights and social status. There is a very strong case for arguing that effective learners need to be active participants in their learning rather than passive recipients, and that pupils need to be committed members of their school community with appropriate levels of responsibility.

Of course, there are sensitivities about the extent of pupil engagement and the appropriateness of their involvement in certain activities. For example, it would be wrong for pupils to be given full responsibility for the appointment of staff or to pass judgement on teachers' effectiveness in the classroom. However, it is entirely appropriate for pupils to be *consulted* about the appointment of new members of staff and to be *consulted* on the effectiveness of teaching and learning.

Key quotes for the section

> The fact is that pupils themselves have a huge contribution to make, not as passive objects but as active players in the education system. Students can and should participate, not only in the construction of their own learning environments, but as research partners in examining questions of learning and anything else that happens in and around schools.
>
> **(Rudduck, 2005: 45)**

> State parties shall assure to the child who is capable of forming his or her own views the right to express those views freely in all matters affecting the child, the views of the child being given due weight in accordance with the age and maturity of the child.
>
> **(United Nations Convention on the Rights of the Child, Article 12)**

G4

> This year, we have started work on involving the children in the SDP [school development plan], so we have elected learning leaders from each class who will create a child version of the school's SDP. They will interview the SMT [senior management team] person in charge of each priority as an initial step to finding out what we are all trying to achieve. It will be written in their own language and with phrases that explain what we are trying to do so that they and their families can understand it easily.
>
> **(Marcelo Staricoff, head of Hertford Infant and Nursery School, Brighton, quoted in ldr, 2013)**

Section discussion (CD-ROM)

The British seem to have a problem in agreeing on the precise status of children. For some they are apprentice adults to be nurtured towards adulthood; for others they are simply immature and need to live in a controlled and structured environment. A third way is surely to see young people as individuals with rights and duties in a democratic society for whom education needs to include opportunities to develop an understanding of what it means to be a member of a community and a citizen. The principles of democracy cannot be taught in the abstract – they have to be experienced and lived. It is a useful exercise to look at how, in practice, your own school views its pupils. Resource G4(i) asks you to list examples of pupil involvement in four different areas and to identify each as one of the three styles outlined above (i.e. apprentice adult, immature adult and democratic participant). Which attitude is most prevalent towards the children?

Another significant factor to consider when debating the possible role and status of pupils is the need to secure their active engagement in learning opportunities within the school. Historically, students have served in schools in monitoring roles (e.g. as prefects supporting staff in the control of other pupils) or in minor organisational roles (e.g. school councils organising student events). Many of today's school leaders gained their first leadership experience by being made responsible for handing out milk or collecting in the pencils! To move things on, the pivotal issue is the balance between consultation and participation; the latter being the real criterion for meaningful engagement.

There are now some very real shifts towards involving pupils in some aspects of the learning of their peers through strategies such as reading buddies, playground play leaders and peer coaching. What remains contentious is engaging pupils in judgements on the appropriateness and effectiveness of their learning experiences – in particular, the impact that their teachers have on their learning. Some would consider that children lack the maturity necessary to make judgements about their teachers and the resulting learning, believing this level of pupil involvement might lessen the authority of teachers.

However, there is growing evidence that for effective learning to occur, learners need to be active participants in the significant decisions pertaining to what and how they learn, and they need to develop the capacity to review the effectiveness of their learning experiences.

This is an issue of mutual respect and trust and, just as importantly, it is about training pupils in the skills and strategies necessary to make a valid and significant contribution. In high trust organisations, children and young people are given opportunities to contribute to every aspect of the life of their community and are able to take on responsibilities appropriate to their level of maturity.

If you are keen to develop pupil engagement within your school, use resource G4(ii) to focus the thoughts of your leadership team. What do you want to improve and why? Perhaps include a selection of pupils in your meetings. Schools that have been brave in this area have found that pupils frequently outperform any expectations and add immense value to the dialogue.

An obvious point, but one worth stressing, is that the principles identified in this discussion need to apply to *all* the adults in the school and not simply to those making the rules.

Key questions

How would you define the attitudes towards pupils in your school: paternalistic/dependency or partnership based on mutual respect?

What evidence is there that pupils are seen as members of a community, are trusted and are given authentic opportunities to serve?

In which areas do pupils have genuine opportunities to make significant choices about their own learning and their involvement across the school?

How real are the responsibilities delegated to pupils?

What training is provided to help pupils to become effective contributors in the leadership and management of the school?

G4

What evidence is there of consistent application of participatory strategies in all classrooms?

Resources (CD-ROM)

G4(i)	Summary of pupils' views
G4(ii)	Implications for student involvement

5   Working across the ages

Question

Does the current education system, comprised of different age related phases, really work to the benefit of pupils?

Why is this important?

Splitting education into age related chunks is an expensive decision for any society; therefore, it must be reasonable to assume that it is the most effective way to deliver learning. For that reason, it is appropriate to investigate the relationship between the phases to see if this system is enhancing or detracting from long term progress.

Key quotes for the section

> The more I live, the more I learn. The more I learn, the more I realize, the less I know.
>
> **(Michel Legrand)**

> Education is not the filling of a pail, but the lighting of a fire.
>
> **(W. B. Yeats)**

> Intellectual growth should commence at birth and cease only at death.
>
> **(Albert Einstein)**

Section discussion (CD-ROM)

When considering a partnership between companies, an argument frequently used is that by working together they produce more than the sum of their parts. Indeed, why would any two organisations work together if this didn't happen? So, is this true for primary and secondary schools? Do they complement the activities of each other? The evidence doesn't look promising. Studies seem to show pupil levels of attainment stalling (or even dipping) as they move between phases of education, and current national accountability measures seem to be driving the sectors even further apart rather than encouraging collaboration.

G5

We give a name to the movement of pupils between primary and secondary school – transition. The word suggests gradual change, a morphing from one form to another; whereas the experience for many young people is anything but gradual and more of a jolt. So, what is transition like in your school? How many days do you allocate to it? What activities do you include and what information do you give (or ask for) in the process? Use resource G5(i) to collect information about the strengths and weaknesses of the process you are involved in.

Sadly, for many schools, the process of working together is squashed into a few days (or, for a small number, a single day), when the reality is that good transition should represent a partnership between schools rather than just a few activities for pupils. For example, some schools are now prioritising only English and maths levels, and a number of secondary schools test new pupils on the first day they visit their new school. These are the behaviours of a dysfunctional system, one that lacks trust, and is not open to working together.

Imagine you were designing an education system from scratch for children aged between 3 and 18. Would you use the template of a primary school and allow the pupils to stay on until they were 18, or a secondary school which allowed the pupils to start at an earlier age? Whatever your answer, the fact that you understand the question, and can see a difference between the two, reinforces the fact that our education system has a problem.

The separate functioning and accountability systems have led most primary and secondary schools to evolve as separate entities with just short annual bridge between the two. This has resulted in a huge diversity in attitudes, teaching methods, environment, language used and large parts of day-to-day practice. Some of the differences may be functions of the ages they serve, but much is simply due to carelessness and a lack of effectively planned collaboration. The effect this has is to alienate many pupils at a time of inevitable stress. In some instances, our lack of care in failing to make this a smooth transition is a temporary setback that the pupil's enthusiasm for their new school will overcome, but for others it marks the beginning of a permanent disengagement with education.

If you are serious about improving the learning experience across the ages in your community, the first step is to get an accurate picture of what the current experience is actually like for pupils. Plan a series of pupil tracking observations across the schools in your partnership, focusing on the year group either side of the transition point. Make the process about the learning experience, not observing the teachers. What is the environment like? How are lessons started/finished? What specialist language is used? What are the classroom walls like? (Resource G5(ii) would be a useful starting point for your tracking.) Carry out the exercise as widely as possible and then transfer the results to resource G5(iii).

You are now in a position to begin building a long term transition programme, not one that is focused on the weeks before the summer term, but one that is about creating a continuity of learning across all ages. Produce a plan for the year, outlining how the schools are going to work together across all aspects of the curriculum to smooth out the learning transition.

Key questions

What do you understand by transition?

Why does your school do the things it does?

Have these strategies been effective in the past?

Do you know how the process affects your pupils?

Resources (CD-ROM)

G5(i)	Transition in your school: a self-review
G5(ii)	Pupil tracking review
G5(iii)	Pupil tracking summary: similarities and differences between schools

Engaging with students, parents and community

1   The family effect – improving understanding to improve collaboration

Question

What are appropriate levels of consultation and participation for families and other school stakeholders?

Why is this important?

The issue of consultation and participation is very closely related to the issue of involvement and engagement. It is a matter of degrees of influence – the ability to make meaningful decisions and to be fully integrated into organisational processes. Consultation is essentially a two-way process of sharing opinions and perspectives, while participation entails active involvement in the making of significant decisions. Involvement implies positive interest, while engagement implies a deeper and longer term commitment.

The challenge for schools is the precise ratio of consultation and participation, and involvement and engagement, for pupils, their parents and the wider community. The crucial issue is the level at which stakeholders become actively involved. The parallel with a company's shareholders is apt – for most of the year shareholders effectively delegate the management of the business to the board, but at times they can become very actively involved. A school's governors should be engaged and participating, but what about the other stakeholders?

The types of parental and community activities in British schools is very much a product of our national culture. For example, norms and expectations with regard to parenting are very different in Reggio Emilia in Italy, as is the role of community values in Finnish education.

H1

Key quotes for the section

> Parental involvement is given a high priority in the Reggio preschools and parents are actively involved not so much as helpers and educators within the schools but within Reggio administration and policymaking. They have a clear 'voice' in the development of the preschools. Many are also involved as 'friends of Reggio children' and those we met articulate the philosophy clearly and understand its practices.
>
> **(Philips, 2001: 60)**

> Finland is, however, very unique among nations in terms of its values, cultural determinants and social cohesion within society. Fairness, honesty and social justice are deeply rooted in the Finnish way of life. People have a strong sense of shared responsibility ...
>
> The intense individuality of Finns blended with low hierarchy and traditional willingness to work with others has opened pathways.
>
> **(Sahlberg, 2011: 10)**

Section discussion (CD-ROM)

While involvement is important, it is engagement that has the greatest potential to make a positive impact on a child's potential for success and well-being. In its simplest form, involvement might be defined as parents responding to the school; engagement is when the school actively responds to parents in order to create a partnership focused on the well-being and success of their child. There is genuine collaboration and cooperation between the school and family. In the Reggio Emilia model of Early Years education, for example, parents are described as 'co-educators'.

It would be useful for your leadership group to consider where your own school sits on the scale between parent co-educators and the parent–school disconnect. Use resource H1(i) to focus your discussion. Recall specific examples of parent–school relationships and decide if they are typical of all or just a smaller group – place them on the continuum provided. Are you happy with the position you have described?

The aspirations of parents reinforce what many involved with the development and education of children have known intuitively for years. In essence, there is no substitute for the highly effective family. There are obvious cultural, social and moral issues directly related to childhood experiences of family life. There are also very real issues of cognitive and neurological development that have profound implications in terms of personal academic potential. The two pivotal factors in determining the effective family are *play*, as the key to socialisation, and *language*, as the basis for all learning. In a review of research from across the world, Desforges and Abouchaar draw very explicit and highly confident conclusions:

> [P]arental involvement in the form of 'at-home good parenting' has a significant positive effect on children's achievement and adjustment even after all other factors shaping attainment have been taken out of the equation. In the primary age range the impact caused by different levels of parental involvement is much bigger than the differences associated with variations in the quality of schools. The scale of the impact is evident across all social classes and all ethnic groups.
>
> **(Desforges and Abouchaar, 2003: 4–5)**

If this is true of parental involvement, then what might parental engagement look like? Equally, if we move from pupil involvement in their learning and school life to pupil engagement, what would have to change? It seems reasonable to argue that the greater the degree of participation, the greater the engagement, and the greater a person's potential to exercise significant choices, the higher the potential level of commitment and motivation.

Use resource H1(ii) to consider your own situation and to articulate your view of the balance between involvement and engagement. Find an example of each category within your school and identify specific ways you could develop work in these areas.

Might there be a case for schools working to move beyond parental participation, as described by Desforges and Abouchaar, to a model much more like the one used in Reggio Emilia? The extent to which the community actively participates in the leadership and life of the school is an indication of local political structures and the nature of the community. In some education systems, the community effectively owns the school (e.g. US school districts and most Scandinavian systems).

With increasing participation comes increasing accountability. The willingness and ability of individuals to increase their level of participation may well be determined by the extent to which they are comfortable with potentially being held to account. There is also the issue of the personal qualities and skills needed to be an effective participant. The response to these concerns might be described as proportional participation – in other words, participation that is appropriate to the individual's role and status. Thus, broad issues around the strategic direction of the school should be open to all because they are a common concern, whereas matters concerning financial planning and staff performance issues should be limited to those with appropriate expertise and knowledge.

Use H1(iii) to list the major strategic decisions made within your school during the past 12 months. For each one, indicate if parents were informed of it or involved in it, and if they could have been more fully involved. Make sure that your development plan for the following year includes strategies for ensuring greater engagement.

Key questions

> Should participation be open to all or restricted to those with a proven commitment to the school?

> Are there aspects of school leadership that should be excluded from any move towards increasing participation?

> How does your school reconcile the rights of parents to be actively engaged with the education of their children with the rights of professionals to make appropriate judgements? (Are there analogies with medicine – the rights of the patient and their relatives versus the rights of the clinician?)

> How strong a voice should the community have in school policy?

Resources (CD-ROM)

H1(i)	Parent–school relationships continuum
H1(ii)	Involvement and engagement
H1(iii)	Parental involvement in school decisions

2   Securing parental and community engagement

Question

How do you ensure that parents and the wider community are part of the school?

Why is this important?

Without community and parental engagement we are in very dangerous territory. There are a number of examples of well-meaning individuals or groups who have tried to replicate their successful schools in very different communities without first checking that this is actually what the community wanted or needed.

Key quotes for the section

> 'Parental engagement' does not always mean the same thing to parents and schools.
>
> **(Martinez and Velazquez, 2000)**

> School-based programmes may alleviate fear if parents can be encouraged to feel comfortable when coming to school; targeted support need not be seen as stigmatising if designed to accord with the needs of parents who have been reluctant to engage.
>
> **(Blewett et al., 2010: 43)**

> At the end of the day, the most overwhelming key to a child's success is the positive involvement of parents.
>
> **(Jane D. Hull)**

Section discussion (CD-ROM)

The effect that parents and community opinions have on the attitude of a child at school should not be underestimated. If a pupil is encouraged to feel negatively about the school, its teachers or its aims, it is extremely unlikely that the child will have the resilience to make long term progress. If a child rushes through the door of their home claiming, 'Those teachers hate me', and is met with agreement, it is doubtful that they will move past their current obstacle to realise that the school (and most of its teachers) are actually trying to support rather than punish. How the school is viewed, and how it thinks it is viewed, are often very different things. If you are feeling brave, try carrying out interviews with key local people who live and work near your school – the local shopkeeper, the librarian, the doctor's receptionist, the milkman, the pub owner, the youth worker. Use questions like those in H2(i) to gain a picture of the way the school is regarded in the community. By focusing on this group, you are more likely to get an honest view rather than a response designed to please or antagonise. Many schools do not have the courage to do this, but unless schools have an accurate idea of how we are actually perceived, developing positive community relationships is far more problematic.

A school in the one of the most deprived areas of northern England employed an anthropologist to spend six months living in the community surrounding the school. She commented that from the moment school finished in July until it opened in September, it was a 'non-topic'. In her opinion, the school was not badly regarded; it just wasn't regarded at all. It had a purely social function for much of the community as a place where children met to interact. Her advice to the school was that if they were serious about improving their relationship with parents, they had to find non-school ways of doing so. By 'non-school' she meant the school should not blindly stumble into the mistake committed by so many others – organising a 'community meeting' in an assembly hall, with the parent placed in a repeat role of their own school days (data based on personal correspondence).

If parents and others in the community are talked down to (or feel that they have been), they are unlikely to believe that their best interests really correspond with those of the school. Focusing on improvements in literacy and attainment may be what the government are interested in, but this may not be a major concern for the community. One school which developed a successful community relationship talked about 'stealth literacy and numeracy' and arranged events whose main functions were to break down any perceived barriers between home and school, as well as ensuring that any other school aims were subtly addressed. Successful examples of this include a variety of social events in the school building, sporting events and fairs/fetes – any activity which does not set the school in the role of an expert or a representative of authority.

If you are keen to develop an effective relationship between your school and its community, the next step could be to use resource H2(ii) to gather ideas about what various community groups require from you and, in turn, how you hope to benefit from them. Attempt to identify activities that could be of benefit to both sides. It is worth recognising that building effective community relationships is a marathon rather than a sprint, and new forms of activity should not be abandoned because your first attempts only attract a low turnout. An excellent event for 15 will produce better long term results than a poor event for 200.

Involve your governors (after all, they *should* represent the community and parents) by giving them the last 12 months' worth of communications to parents (newsletters etc.) and asking them to provide honest feedback using a form such as the one in resource H2(iii). Some schools are using new technologies to great effect – for example, using video newsletters and even embedded QR codes which reveal pupils talking about their work. In this way, pupils are far more likely to use language appropriate to their community and should become a bridge between, rather than an obstacle to, home–school relationships. Don't let your communication with home be an afterthought in the last week of term – make it a key part of your school development plan.

Key questions

Do you really know what the community thinks of your school?

Does the school act like a 'school' in events which involve the community?

Do you view the community as central to all you do or as an obstacle to be overcome?

When did you last completely review your communications with home?

Do you make the most of modern technologies in your relationships with parents?

Resources (CD-ROM)

H2(i)	Questionnaire for local community figures
H2(ii)	Community and school needs
H2(iii)	Governor review of home–school communication

3   The community as a resource

Question

In what ways can a school engage with its community to their mutual benefit?

Why is this important?

Not so many years ago, most teachers would live in the community that their school served and would have a direct interest in engaging with that community and building strong relationships. This is rarely the case today, so schools have to work even harder to create durable school–community links. These relationships potentially have a twofold impact. First, there is a high correlation between living in an effective community and academic success. Second, from a broader educational perspective, it is important that the school sees the wider community as a valid and significant resource to support learning and as an element of wider educational outcomes (e.g. citizenship, community service, well-being and making a contribution to society).

Any model of effective teaching and learning, including a school's curriculum, needs to demonstrate a direct and explicit engagement with the community as both a relevant resource for learning and as a means of embedding the school in the life of the community.

Key quotes for the section

> Reweaving social webs will depend in part on the efforts of dedicated local leaders who choose to pursue their goals … through the sometimes slow, frequently fractious, and profoundly transformative route of social capital building. But reweaving will also depend on our ability to create new spaces for recognition, reconnection, conversation and debate.
>
> **(Putnam, 2003: 294)**

> Never doubt that a small group of thoughtful, committed citizens can change the world. Indeed, it's the only thing that ever has.
>
> **(Margaret Mead)**

Section discussion (CD-ROM)

A school exists because of its community, and in the highest performing education systems there is often a very strong link between the school and its geographical environment.

In England, we seem to be moving away from the idea that the community actually owns the school, but that does not diminish the importance and potential significance of schools to community engagement, cooperation and working to mutual advantage.

A good starting point for leaders is to look at your own website and school brochure. Is this a lively representation of the work you do with your community? Does it act as a catalyst or a barrier to further development? Use H3(i) as the basis for your analysis and as a focus for the next steps. If you are feeling brave, ask someone from outside the school to complete it too.

School–community interactions can be split into three broad areas:

1   The community as a resource to enhance the curriculum and teaching and learning:
    → Coaches and mentors from across the community.
    → Work experience and shadowing.
    → Living history projects (within the curriculum and beyond).

2   Working with the community to enhance student engagement and well-being:
    → Family liaison workers.
    → Programmes to support parenting.
    → Healthy lifestyle projects.

3   Contributing to community development projects:
    → Volunteering on community improvement projects (e.g. play spaces).
    → Working with vulnerable groups.
    → Working on behalf of local charities.

Use H3(ii) to analyse your current work with the community and to identify your priorities for the next stage of your development.

For the links between school and community to be successful, a number of factors need to be in place. First, there needs to be a careful analysis of the structural conditions. These are the factors that are available to support an initiative – for example, the availability of resources from a range of sources and the use of existing policies and strategies to underpin a community project. Second, networks need to be established by 'nesting' smaller groups within larger groups to create an enhanced a sense of belonging and commitment and to foster personal relationships. Third, a sense of interdependence between school and community should be created by developing an overarching and collective sense of belonging through the development of common purpose and shared values. Finally, multi-stranded networks of shared interests and common concerns will

H3

ensure that communication is open and transparent. Resource H3(iii) is offered as a starting point for developing community work using these four steps.

Successful schools recognise that developing strong community connections is not an afterthought to be completed once the main job is done. The community can serve as a resource to the extent that there is mutual respect and genuine reciprocity, with two-way benefits and everybody winning.

Key questions

What evidence do you have about the way in which the community perceives the school?

What status does your school documentation give to links with the community?

How are community relations managed in terms of staffing and resources?

Who is responsible for managing the links between school and community?

Resources (CD-ROM)

H3(i)	How community focused is your outward image?
H3(ii)	The types of community interaction within your school
H3(iii)	School–community project plan

4   Win-win models of collaboration

Question

How can a partnership be grown that benefits all sides?

Why is this important?

Schools are repeatedly being told to look outside their own four walls to broaden the pupils' experience. If the relationships can be structured to last, and become a meaningful part of the curriculum, this must be the ideal. Relationships are far more likely to be long lasting if the partner benefits as much as the school.

Key quotes for the section

> The Law of Win/Win says, 'Let's not do it your way or my way; let's do it the best way.'
>
> **(Greg Anderson)**

> If you can't go around it, over it, or through it, you had better negotiate with it.
>
> **(Ashleigh Brilliant)**

> Unless both sides win, no agreement can be permanent.
>
> **(Jimmy Carter)**

Section discussion (CD-ROM)

Relationships of any kind are far more likely to succeed if both sides are fundamentally committed to them. This is as true for educational partnerships as it is for romantic liaisons. The educational equivalent of a one night stand, an event where a partner swoops in to support a school on a single occasion, is unlikely to provide long term advantages.

A good start for any relationship is to discuss mutual benefits from the initial meeting. Resource H4(i) blown up to A3 offers an effective tool to brainstorm why all sides might want to be involved in the partnership. It prompts participants to consider what is in it for them, the pupils and the wider community. A rule of thumb would be to aim for roughly equal benefits for each group. Any more than this and the project is moving into self-interest; any less and there is a danger of the partner losing interest. Many potential partners are at first wrong-footed by the question, 'What is in it for you?' But once they realise that you are asking this because you are keen to form a long lasting relationship, the most imaginative are likely to focus on how best to work with you.

Some schools can be seduced into receiving 'gifts' from external bodies, and given the tightening of budgets this is understandable, but this must not be confused with partnership. Genuine partnership should be of long term value to both sides.

A few possible benefits are shown in the table below:

Pupils	Community	Partners
Improved curriculum relevance	Increased opportunities	Motivation for workforce
External visits	Work experience	Real tasks completed by pupils
Mentoring (in person or electronically)	Opportunities for involvement with school	Opportunity to be involved in education
Projects in the real world	External validation of work	Improved public relations

We have seen examples of schools that have formed such close relationships with a company that the projects weave into every aspect of the curriculum and are a natural part of the school and partner's life. For example, the languages department producing handbooks for foreign workers, the design and technology department designing and constructing safety signs, the English department producing the programme for a major conference, and the ICT department acting as a training venue for elementary lessons in Word or Excel (run by pupils). Some leaders might worry that these examples represent enforced child labour. If the school is simply becoming a cheap 'fix it' solution for the company, this would be a valid objection. However, if the projects are designed as an enhancement to the existing curriculum, then the pupils are given a real context for their work and the pride of seeing that their output is considered worthy by the 'adult' world. This win-win attitude works not only with business but also between educational establishments – examples range from imaginative work experience with a local nursery to a university archaeology department that develops placements in secondary schools as part of its undergraduate course.

If you are keen to form exceptional partnerships, the first step is to make a list of the areas of your current work that would benefit from external input. Resource H4(ii) provides a foundation for this analysis. Use this to analyse your curriculum and consider topics that would benefit from external support. You now have a shopping list. Ask the potential partner to produce a similar list for themselves. Look at the two side by side and identify initial areas that could cover both sets of needs. Once you have identified a couple of potential areas for collaboration, produce a project grid to clarify the expectations of both partners (see H4(iii)). Win-win relationships need constant review and nurturing to ensure that the needs of both sides are being met, but the benefits for everyone are often far greater than the original expectations.

Key questions

Can the school do everything it needs from within the school?

Why do you want to work with someone from outside?

What can they bring that would be useful to the school? What can you bring to them?

Are you nurturing the relationship to make sure it is effective for both parties?

Resources (CD-ROM)

H4(i)	Rule of three for effective partnership
H4(ii)	Identifying the gaps
H4(iii)	Partnership project planning grid

References and further reading

Alarcon, G. M., Edwards, J. M. and Menke, L. E. (2011). Student Burnout and Engagement: A Test of the Conservation of Resources Theory, *Journal of Psychology: Interdisciplinary and Applied* 145(3): 211–227.

Anderson, G. L., Herr, K. and Nihlen, A. (2007). *Studying Your Own School: An Educator's Guide to Practitioner Action Research*, 2nd edn. Thousand Oaks, CA: Corwin Press.

Association of School and College Leaders (ASCL) (2012). *Intelligent Accountability*. Policy Paper 86. Leicester: ASCL.

Barber, M., Whelan, F. and Clark, M. (2010). *Capturing the Leadership Premium: How the World's Top School Systems Are Building Leadership Capacity for the Future.* N.p.: McKinsey & Company. Available at: http://mckinseyonsociety.com/downloads/reports/Education/schoolleadership_final.pdf.

Barkley, E. F. (2010). *Student Engagement Techniques: A Handbook for College Faculty* (Higher and Adult Education Series). San Francisco, CA: Jossey-Bass.

Battle, M. (2009). *Ubuntu: I in You and You in Me.* New York: Seabury Books.

Bennis, W. G. and Nanus, A. (1985). *Leadership: The Strategies for Taking Charge.* New York: Collins.

Blewett, J., Noble, J. and Tunstill, J. (2010). *Improving the Safety, Health and Wellbeing of Children through Improving the Physical and Mental Health of Mothers, Fathers and Carers* (Families, Parents and Carers Research Review 1). London: C4EO. Available at: http://socialwelfare.bl.uk/subject-areas/services-client-groups/children-young-people/c4eo/126008physical_mental_health_research_review.pdf.

Bolam, R., McMahon, A., Stoll, L., et al. (2005). *Creating and Sustaining Effective Professional Learning Communities.* Research Report No. 637. Nottingham: DfES. Available at: http://www.educationscotland.gov.uk/Images/Creating%20and%20Sustaining%20PLCs_tcm4-631034.pdf.

Bolman, L. G. and Deal, T. E. (2013). *Reframing Organizations: Artistry, Choice, and Leadership,* 5th edn. San Francisco, CA: Jossey-Bass.

Brady, L. (1985). *Models and Methods of Teaching.* Sydney: Prentice-Hall of Australia.

Bryk, A. S. and Schneider, B. (2002). *Trust in Schools: A Core Resource for Improvement* (American Sociological Association's Rose Series in Sociology). New York: Russell Sage Foundation.

Bryk, A. S., Sebring, P. B., Allensworth, E., Luppescu, S. and Easton, J. Q. (2010). *Organizing Schools for Improvement: Lessons from Chicago*. Chicago, IL: University of Chicago Press.

Covey, S. R. (1992). *Principle-Centered Leadership*. London: Simon & Schuster.

Department for Education (DfE) (2010). *The Importance of Teaching: The Schools White Paper*. Norwich: TSO. Available at: https://www.gov.uk/government/uploads/system/uploads/attachment_data/file/175429/CM-7980.pdf.

Department for Education (DfE) (2013). *Teachers' Standards: Guidance for School Leaders, School Staff and Governing Bodies, July 2011 (introduction updated June 2013)*. Available at: https://www.gov.uk/government/uploads/system/uploads/attachment_data/file/301107/Teachers__Standards.pdf.

Department of Education (Northern Ireland) (n.d.). *Community Use of School Premises: A Guidance Toolkit for Schools*. Available at: http://www.deni.gov.uk/index/schools-and-infrastructure-2/community-use-of-schools/community_use_of_schools_guidance_toolkit.htm.

Desforges, C. with Abouchaar, A. (2003). *The Impact of Parental Involvement, Parental Support and Family Education on Pupil Achievement and Adjustment: A Literature Review*. DfES Research Report 433. Available at: http://www.creativitycultureeducation.org/wp-content/uploads/impact-of-parental-involvement-parental-support.pdf.

Fullan, M. (2010). *All Systems Go: The Change Imperative for Whole System Reform*. Thousand Oaks, CA: Corwin Press.

Gardner, H. (2006). *Five Minds for the Future*. Boston, MA: Harvard Business School Press.

Gawande, A. (2011). *The Checklist Manifesto: How to Get Things Right*. London: Profile Books.

Goleman, D., Boyatzis, R. E. and McKee, A. (2002). *The New Leaders: Transforming the Art of Leadership*. London: Little, Brown.

Groves, M. (2008). *Regenerating Schools*. London: Network Continuum.

Gunter, M. A., Estes, T. H. and Schwab, J. (2003). *Instruction: A Models Approach*, 4th edn. Boston, MA: Allyn and Bacon.

Haberman, M. (2013). Why School Culture Matters, and How to Improve It, *Huffington Post* (10 April). Available at: http://www.huffingtonpost.com/Michael-Haberman/why-school-culture-matter_b_3047318.html.

Hall, L. M. with Duval, M. and Dilts, R. (2003). *Coaching Conversations*. Clifton, CO: Neuro-Semantics Publications.

Handy, C. (1994). *The Age of Paradox*. Boston, MA: Harvard Business School Press.

Hargreaves, A. and Fink, D. (2006). *Sustainable Leadership*. San Francisco, CA: Jossey-Bass.

Hargreaves, A. and Fullan, M. (2012). *Professional Capital: Transforming Teaching in Every School*. London: Routledge.

Hargreaves, A. and Harris, A. (2011). *Performance Beyond Expectations*. Nottingham: NCSL.

Hargreaves, A. and Shirley, D. (2009). *The Fourth Way: The Inspiring Future for Educational Change*. Thousand Oaks, CA: Corwin Press.

Hargreaves, D. H. (2010). *Creating a Self-Improving School System*. Nottingham: NCSL.

ldr (2013). Leadership Interview: Creating Confident Young Learners, *ldr magazine* (autumn). Available at: http://www.nationalcollege.org.uk/index/resources/ldr-magazine/back-ldr-issues/ldr-autumn-2013/leadership-interview-creating-confident-young-learners.htm.

Leadbeater, C. (2003). Open Innovation in Public Services, in T. Bentley and J. Wilsdon (eds), *The Adaptive State: Strategies for Personalising the Public Realm*. London: Demos, pp. 37–49.

Leithwood, K., Day, C., Sammons, P., Harris, A. and Hopkins D. (2006). *Seven Strong Claims about Successful School Leadership*. Nottingham: NCSL.

Marshall, S. P. (1995). The Vision, Meaning, and Language of Educational Transformation: How Chaos, Complexity, Theory, and Flocking Behavior Can Inform Leadership in Transition. Available at: http://www.stephaniepacemarshall.com/articles/SPM-Article8.pdf.

Martinez, Y. G. and Velazquez, J. A. (2000). Involving Migrant Families in Education. *Eric Digest,* ERIC Clearinghouse on Rural Education and Small Schools. Available at: http://www.ericdigests.org/2001-3/migrant.htm.

Maslow, A. H. (1966). *The Psychology of Science: A Reconnaissance*. Chicago, IL: Regnery.

Megill, K. A. (2013). *Thinking for a Living: The Coming Age of Knowledge Work*. Berlin: Walter de Gruyter.

Menter, I. J., Elliot, D., Hulme, M., Lewin, J. and Lowden, K. (2011). *A Guide to Practitioner Research in Education*. London: SAGE.

Moreno, J. M., Mulford, B. and Hargreaves, A. (2006). *Trusting Leadership: From Standards to Social Capital*. Nottingham: NCSL. Available at: http://www.nationalcollege.org.uk/docinfo?id=17443&filename=trusting-leadership.pdf.

Morrison, K. (2002). *School Leadership and Complexity Theory*. London: RoutledgeFalmer.

Novak, J. (2008). Inviting Passionate Educational Leadership, in B. Davies and T. Brighouse (eds), *Passionate Leadership in Education*. London: Sage, pp. 35–56.

Ofsted (2012). *Getting to Good*. Ref: 120167. London: Ofsted. Available at: http://www.ofsted.gov.uk/sites/default/files/documents/surveys-and-good-practice/g/Getting%20to%20good.pdf.

Opetusalan Ammattijärjestö (OAJ) (n.d.). *The Teacher's Professional Ethics*. Helsinki: OAJ.

Perkins, D. N. (1981). *The Mind's Best Work*. Cambridge, MA: Harvard University Press.

Phillips, S. (2001). Special Needs or Special Rights?, in L. Abbot and C. Nutbrown (eds), *Experiencing Reggio Emilia: Implications for Pre-School Provision*. Buckingham: Open University Press, pp. 48–61.

Pont, B., Nusche, D. and Hopkins, D. (eds) (2014). *Improving School Leadership*. Vol. 2: *Case Studies on System Leadership*. Paris: OECD.

Preskill, S., Vermilya, L. and Otero, G. (2000). *Skills for Democracy: Promoting Dialogue in Schools*. Victoria, Australia: Hawker Brownlow Education.

PricewaterhouseCoopers (2007). *Independent Study into School Leadership*. Nottingham: DfES.

Putnam, R. (2003). *Better Together: Restoring the American Community*. New York: Simon & Schuster.

Robinson, K. (2001). *Out of Our Minds: Learning to be Creative*. Oxford: Capstone.

Robinson, K. (2006). *How Schools Kill Creativity* (video). Available at: http://www.ted.com/talks/ken_robinson_says_schools_kill_creativity.

Robinson, V. M. J. (2011). *Student-Centered Leadership*. San Francisco, CA: Jossey-Bass.

Rudduck, J. (2005). Pupil Voice is Here to Stay. QCA Futures project paper. Available at: http://www.serviceschoolsmobilitytoolkit.com/resourcedownloads/staffroom/bpv_theneedtoinvolvepupilvoice.pdf.

Sahlberg, P. (2011). *Finnish Lessons: What Can the World Learn from Educational Change in Finland?* New York: Teachers' College Press.

Schlechty, P. C. (2002). *Working on the Work: An Action Plan for Teachers, Principals, and Superintendents*. San Francisco, CA: Jossey-Bass.

Sebba, J. and Robinson, C. (2010). *Evaluation of UNICEF UK's Rights Respecting School Award*. London: UNICEF.

Shell (2008). Preparing for the Future, in *Competitive Strategies for Winning in the Downturn* (Sponsored Supplement). Available at: http://s02.staticshell.com/content/dam/shell/static/globalsolutions/downloads/aboutshell/special-supplements/preparing-for-thefuture.pdf.

Smith, A. (2011). *High Performers: The Secrets of Successful Schools*. Carmarthen: Crown House Publishing.

Southworth, G. (2004). *Primary School Leadership in Context: Leading Small, Medium, and Large Sized Schools*. London: RoutledgeFalmer.

Spellings, M. (2005). Seeing the Data, Meeting the Challenge. Speech given at the Indiana High School Summit: Redesigning Indiana's High Schools, 14 June.

Sternberg, R. J. (1990). *Wisdom: Its Nature, Origins, and Development*. Cambridge: Cambridge University Press.

Sternberg, R. J. (2005). A Model of Educational Leadership: Wisdom, Intelligence and Creativity Synthesized, *International Journal of Leadership in Education* 8(4): 347–364.

Taffinder, P. (1998). *Big Change*. Chichester: John Wiley.

Waters, M. (2013). *Thinking Allowed on Schooling*. Carmarthen: Independent Thinking Press.

West-Burnham, J. (n.d.). Understanding Deep Learning, *John West-Burnham*. Available at: http://www.johnwest-burnham.co.uk/index.php/understanding-deep-learning.

West-Burnham, J., Farrar, M. and Otero, G. (2007). *Schools and Communities: Working Together to Transform Children's Lives*. London: Network Continuum.

Zeldin, T. (1998). *Conversation: How Talk Can Change Your Life*. London: Harvill Press.

CD-ROM menu

A Effective leadership

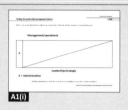

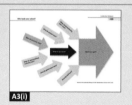

A5 Creating school cultures — 19

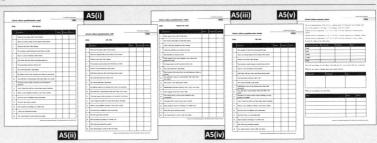

A5(i) · A5(ii) · A5(iii) · A5(iv) · A5(v)

A6 Accountability — 22

A6(i) · A6(ii) · A6(iii)

B Thinking strategically

B1 From improvement to transformation — 25

B1(i) · B1(ii) · B1(iii)

B2 Leading through vision — 29

B2(i) · B2(ii) · B2(iii)

B3 Developing future scenarios

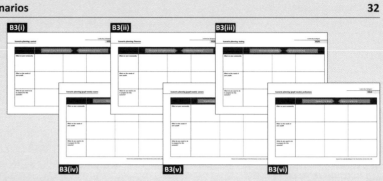
B4 Exploring alternative futures

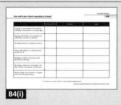

B5 Spiral thinking

C Leading innovation and change

C1 Leading through creativity

C2 Creating a research and inquiry based culture 47

C2(i)

C2(ii)

C3 Organisational change and personal change 50

C3(i)

C4 Encouraging risk taking 53

C4(i)

C4(ii)

C4(ii)

C5 Structure vs. freedom 56

C5(i)

C5(ii)

C5(iii)

D Leading teaching and learning

D1 Equity, fairness, vulnerable students and closing the gap   59

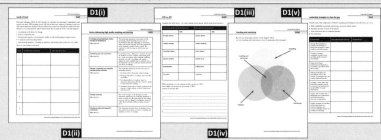

D2 Leading dialogue about teaching and learning   62

D3 Securing learner engagement   66

D4 Models of learning   70

D4(i)
D4(ii)
D4(iii)

D5 Models of teaching 74

D5(i)

D5(ii)

D6 Improving teaching and learning 77

D6(i)

D6(ii)

D6(iii)

E Leading and managing resources

E1 Prevention is better than cure 81

E1(i)

E2 Procedures and systems 84

E2(i)

E2(ii)

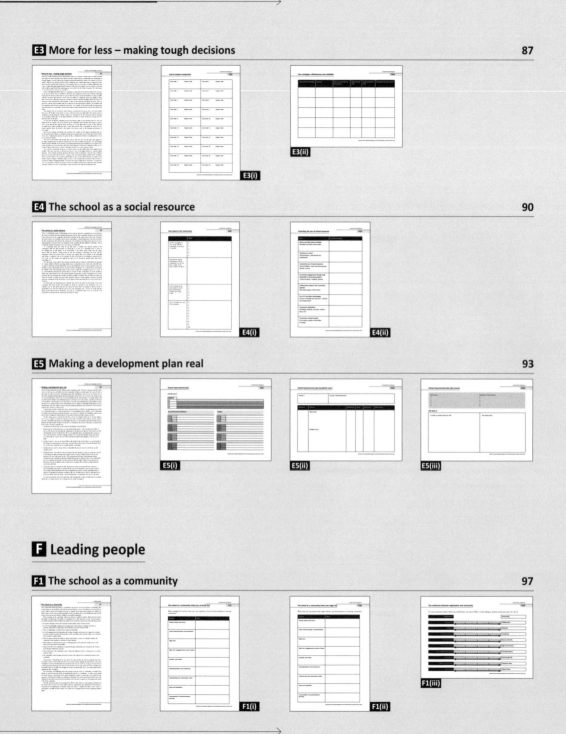

F2 Leading through trust 101

F2(i)

F2(ii)

F3 Challenging conversations 104

F3(i)

F3(ii)

F4 Effective continuing professional development 109

F4(i)

F4(ii)

F5 Shared leadership 112

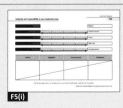
F5(i)

F5(ii)

G Collaboration

G1 Reconciling autonomy and collaboration   117

 G1(i)
 G1(ii)

G2 Strategies for collaborative working   120

 G2(i)
 G2(ii)

G3 Sustaining the school while working in the system   124

 G3(i)

G4 Pupils as partners in learning   127

 G4(i)
 G4(ii)

G5 Working across the ages — 131

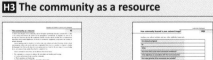

G5(i) G5(ii) G5(iii)

H Engaging with students, parents and community

H1 The family effect – improving understanding to improve collaboration — 135

H1(i) H1(ii) H1(iii)

H2 Securing parental and community engagement — 139

H2(i) H2(ii) H2(iii)

H3 The community as a resource — 142

H3(i) H3(ii) H3(iii)

H4 Win-win models of collaboration

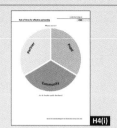

H4(i)

H4(ii)

H4(iii)